Essential
Tunisia

by
MICHAEL TOMKINSON

Michael Tomkinson is a travel author who writes on
Tunisia, Kenya, The Gambia, Uganda and the United
Arab Emirates.
A former Arabist with HM Diplomatic Service, he has
a home in Tunisia.

AA

Produced by AA Publishing

Written by Michael Tomkinson
Verified by Diana Darke
Peace and Quiet section
by Paul Sterry

Reprinted Apr 1998
Revised third edition 1997
Reprinted 1995
Revised second edition 1994
Reprinted 1993
First published 1990

Edited, designed and produced by
AA Publishing.
© The Automobile Association
Maps © The Automobile
Association

Distributed in the United Kingdom
by AA Publishing, Norfolk House,
Priestley Road, Basingstoke,
Hampshire, RG24 9NY.

A CIP catalogue record for this
book is available from the British
Library.

ISBN 0 7495 1337 3

Published by AA Publishing, which
is a trading name of Automobile
Association Developments Limited,
whose registered office is Norfolk
House, Priestley Road, Basingstoke,
Hampshire, RG24 9NY.

Registered number 1878835.

Colour Origination by L C Repro &
Sons Ltd., Aldermaston, England

Printed by: Printers Trento srl, Italy

Cover picture: *Hammamet, from the
ramparts of the kasba*

Contents

This book employs a simple
rating system to help choose
which places to visit:

✓	'top ten'

◆◆◆ do not miss
◆◆ see if you can
◆ worth seeing if you
   have time

Country Distinguishing Signs
On several maps, international
distinguishing signs have been
used to indicate the location of
the countries which surround
Tunisia. Thus:

 = Algeria 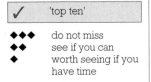 = Libya

The minaret of the Great Mosque viewed from the splendid rooftop terrace of the Palais d'Orient, in Tunis Medina, the old heart of the city

INTRODUCTION

Tunisia is the most sophisticated, tolerant and relaxed state in North Africa. This one-time lair of the Barbary pirates, ex-French protectorate and 'Land of the Veil' first revealed itself to tourism in the mid-1960s. Within a decade it had won a permanent place in most travel agents' programmes, and now over 600 hotels house, feed, transport and entertain an annual average of 4 million visitors.

Writing an up-to-date book about Tunisia is like trying to paint a kaleidoscope or the portrait of an acrobat in action. For this is not only – headlong – a 'developing nation': its stumbling sprint through several stages of social and economic progress simultaneously is also, for the Westerner, somewhat bewildering. The grass-roots growth – begun under ex-president Bourguiba continues – new settlements and suburbs, clinics, schools and low-cost homes – but with the 1980s and 1990s came a spate of more prestige projects including motorways and two new tram-cum-railways, nationwide industrial zones, city-centre skyscrapers, dams, canals and international pipelines, lavish tourist complexes, pleasure ports and more international airports.

The development, though, is not all taking place beneath your hotel bedroom window. The miles of Mediterranean coastline remain for the most part unspoiled and the African sun – one thing safely impervious to Progress – shines most days of the year on blissful beaches, mountains and desert.

BACKGROUND

BACKGROUND

Tunis: a hectic, modern capital and a place where time can stand still

The Place

Tunisia is the northernmost country of Africa and the size of England and Wales – 63,378 square miles (164,150sq km). It backs on to Algeria and the Atlas Mountains in the west, and faces east with a mostly low Mediterranean coast scalloped by the three large gulfs of Tunis, Hammamet and Gabes. With the Algerian frontier very roughly parallel to the eastern seaboard, the average east–west width is 150 miles (240km). The short north coast rises to the Cap Blanc promontory by Bizerta, and the Saharan frontier-post of Borj el Hattaba lies 500 miles (800km) due south, at the point of a long desert prong.

Along the north coast runs the panhandle of a rugged mountain chain, from the Aïn Draham forests of cork-oak and pine to the twin lakes of Bizerta and Ichkeul.

Southwards, the meandering and very fertile Mejerda Valley divides this region from the undulating farmlands of the central Tell (the 'Plateau'). To the east the Tell peters out, firstly into low wheat country that stretches from Bizerta to Tunis, the capital; then, beyond the 'corridor' that leads down to Hammamet, into Cap Bon; finally into the Sahel (the 'Shore') of Sousse. To the south and west the Tell rises into the Dorsale range, Tunisia's 'backbone'.

From the well-watered Mediterranean north, Tunisia then sinks, unevenly, towards the Sahara. In the centre is the steppe region, rich only in Roman remains, interrupted in the west by Jebel Chambi (5,066 feet/1,544m and the country's highest peak) and merging in the east with the unbroken miles of olive-groves that are the Sahel of Sfax. A line of arid hills across from Metlaoui to Maknassy makes one last stand before the desert.

There is a scattering of islands round the 810-mile (1,300km) coast, some little known and uninhabited, others as popular as Jerba.

The Tunisian Sahara starts with curious salt-flats/lakes which are known as *chotts*. On terra firma between them stand the oases: exotic, on-shore islands consisting of palms, pools, camels, beduin and general picturesqueness that not even glossy travel brochures can exaggerate.

There is one more fascinating diversion: the dramatic rise of the Matmatas and the Ksour – bald, russet, mostly table-top summits that shelter Berber cave-dwellers, pit-dwellers and cliff-dwellers. Then the dunes take over. With little more of interest save the name – Great Eastern Erg – Tunisia runs out in the sands of the Sahara.

The People

Tunisia has, since earliest times, been a meeting-place of Middle Eastern and Mediterranean peoples and subject at certain periods to large-scale European penetration. Most of the more determined invasions – Phoenician, Roman, Vandal, Byzantine, Arab, Norman, Spanish, Turkish and finally French – were followed by periods of settlement. The result is skins that range through most colours of the dermal spectrum and which bear witness to the fact that the invading armies, whether Scipio's or Earl Alexander's, have left behind them not only destruction.

The Berbers

Tunisia's aborigines were the Berbers, about whom a great deal has been written but little is known. What few reliable findings there are suggest a typically colourful beginning: that about 10,000 BC a dark-haired, brown-skinned people settled in and around Tunisia to interbreed with both Negroes from the Sahara and mysterious, blue-eyed, blond-haired immigrants from the north. The variegated offspring called themselves *Imazighen* (Noble Ones) but the Romans called them *Barbari* (Uncouth) and this name has, perhaps unjustly, stuck (in *Berber* and *Barbary Coast* but not *Barber*).

When not united in opposition, the Berber tribes took refuge from foreign aggressors on islands like Jerba, in the remoter mountain fastnesses of the Matmatas and the Ksour or behind the lines in isolated, easily defended eagle's nests such as Jeradou, Zriba and Takrouna. The lapse of time may entitle historians to speculate on what centurions, crusaders, *condottieri*, janissaries and even British troops did with the Berber girls, but the evidence we have today is clearer and far more discreet: Arabian, Greek and Levantine profiles, Semitic, Jewish and Roman noses, eyes like those of Sophia Loren, Robert Morley or Omar Sharif. At the last national census the population numbered almost 9 million and constituted a problem. With 55 per cent

BACKGROUND

aged less than 20, 90 per cent of school-age children now being educated (at a cost of one third of the country's budget), and the percentage of adult employment significantly undisclosed, family planning is a crucial economic issue.

A concerted (and often ingenious) government campaign has, however, resulted in Tunisia's now being considered by the UN 'a model for Africa of successful birth control'.

In the towns, especially, the mixture of races results in surprisingly widespread good looks, bright minds and attractive personalities. European and American visitors to this 'developing' country are repeatedly taken aback by children who speak Arabic as their mother tongue, are often bilingual in French by their mid-teens and often go on to fluency in English, German or Italian.

The Past

● **Prehistoric** When North Africa was savanna and swamp and its fauna the big game of Kenya today – one million years before Christ – the first human type appeared in Tunisia. Knowing how to shape stones, he has been accredited with the 'Pebble Culture'.

Many specimens of both this and later, true Stone Age cultures have been found in southern and western Tunisia. Tunisia's first known *Homo*, the Capsian Man, chipped blades and scrapers. Neolithic immigrants from the then green Sahara brought arrows and

fixed agriculture, but remained ignorant of metals until Bronze Age cultures were introduced from Sicily.

● **Punic** Tunisia enters history proper with the Phoenicians, who developed a commercial empire and for this needed regular naval bases. These they established at *Outih* (Utica), *Hadrumetum* (Sousse), *Hippo Diarrhytus* (Bizerta) and *Thines* (Tunis).

When the Assyrians invaded their homeland many Phoenicians fled westwards, and the story of this refugee movement has crystallised round Dido. Elissa was the sister of King Pygmalion of Tyre, who coveted her husband Acherbas' fortune. When Pygmalion had Acherbas killed, Elissa fled with those Tyrians opposed to the king: first to Cyprus, then on to Tunisia. Hereafter history calls Elissa 'Dido'.

The immigrants founded Carthage (*Kart Hadasht* or 'New Capital') in 814 BC. The local ruler Iarbus, the story goes, agreed to their occupying 'as much land as could be covered by the hide of a bull', whereupon Dido's men killed the largest bull, cut its hide into the thinnest shreds and stretched them all the way round what became the Hill of Byrsa (*byrsa*, in Greek, meaning hide). Iarbus then set his sights on Dido. She declined, risked the survival of her people by rebuffing him and solved the dilemma by mounting the epic funeral pile. It is Virgil, 700 years later, who pairs her with Aeneas,

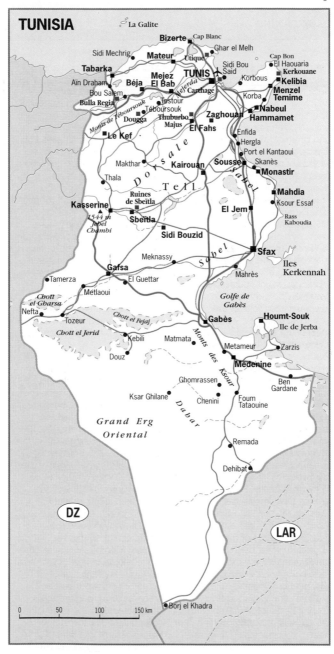

BACKGROUND

overlooking the fact that to have called at Carthage the Trojan hero must have lived to be over 400 years old.

There were centuries of rivalry with the Greeks, also seafaring and pressing westward, but Carthage flourished. Monuments, tombs and *tophets* (crematoria) indicate that, at home, Carthaginian – Punic – control spread from present-day Tabarka to Sfax, and inland to Dougga and Makthar. The Carthaginians built cities which the Romans were to inherit, and marked the countryside with the Levantine system of terracing, which today explains why the slopes of the Atlas look in places like those of the Lebanon.

Most of the archaeological evidence we have is of the Punic dead: the Romans obliterated almost every trace of Carthage, but the dead survived as a clue to the Punic way of life. The *tophets* in Salammbo and Sousse contain the ashes of hundreds of murdered children, strangled in sacrifice to the gods in times of national or personal misfortune.

The 'spectacular' Punic Wars are the best-known part of Carthage's past. The First Punic War (264-241 BC) consisted mainly of naval engagements around Sicily: the Romans for the first time took to the waves and beat the veteran Punic fleet at Milazzo. Rome triumphed again in 241 BC, forcing the Phoenicians out of Sicily and imposing heavy reparations.

Desperate for new sources of

wealth, the Carthaginians turned to Spain. Within 20 years the Barcide rulers had established there an influential kingdom. From northern Spain, in the Second Punic War (218–201 BC), Hannibal led his 59,000 men and 37 elephants over the Alps. He came close to taking Rome but was brought back to Africa by Scipio's advances and then defeated at Zama.

The Third Punic War is a pathetic story of forced suicide. For over half of the 2nd century BC, and with the help of the Berbers, Rome held Carthage in submission. She was regarded as a vassal state of Rome, but remained a thorn in Rome's side, and in the Roman Senate Cato called for her destruction.

In 149 BC the Senate ordered the Carthaginians to abandon their city and move inland. Predictably they refused. The Romans besieged them for almost three years. Strabo wrote that there were 700,000 inside the walls when the siege began: 50,000 were alive when it ended. For over 10 days the starving Carthaginians were slowly forced back up Byrsa Hill. Each house became a battleground. As the hand-to-hand combat forced the occupants upstairs, the Romans demolished or set fire to the rooms below. After seven days of this the 50,000 survivors surrendered and were allowed to leave the burning city. The holocaust closed in on the Temple of Eshmun, atop the Hill of Byrsa, where King Hasdrubal was

encircled with his family and
the remnants of his people.
When the king asked Scipio for
mercy, his people turned
against him and set fire to the
temple that sheltered them.
The fighting then lulled.
Hasdrubal's wife Sophonisbe
thanked Scipio for his
clemency, cursed her husband
as a coward and walked back
into the flames.

● **Roman** Scipio had every
building in Carthage
demolished, the land ploughed
over and sown with salt to
make it barren. Twenty-four
years later, Caius Gracchus
proposed a new city but,
according to Plutarch, the
Roman flag fell down and the
sacrificial animals ran away in
the storm that promptly
followed. Only after Julius
Caesar had routed Pompey's
army in Tunisia, in 46 BC, was
Carthage rebuilt.

Once the Berber kings had
been subdued, Tunisia was
placed under direct Senate
control.

With the Roman empire came
Christianity. It was largely
this that led to the collapse of
Latin Tunisia – Christianity and
the camel. For while the
orthodox church was rife with
schisms, the spread of the
camel in the Sahara gave the
Berbers a mobility that the
Roman legions could not match.
Weakened internally by
religious and social unrest and
externally by these southern
raiders, Tunisia offered little
resistance to the Vandals.

● **Vandal and Byzantine** As the
Vandals inscribed, built and
buried almost nothing, little is

The fall of Carthage to Rome

known about them. Historians
aver that they came in from
Spain in the 420s. From their
showing elsewhere it is
probably safe to assume that
the Vandals contributed
nothing of value to the country.
When, in AD 533, the Byzantine
emperor Justinian sent General
Belisarius to regain Tunisia for
the Eastern Roman Empire, the
Vandal king Gelimir was easily
defeated.

The Byzantines assumed the
mantle of Rome. They occupied
the cities as far west as Haidra
and south to Jerba but,
harassed by the Berbers
throughout their 140-year
occupation, the Byzantines
remained on the defensive.

● **Arab** It was as much the
resurgent Berbers as the
declining Byzantines that stood
in the path of the Muslim
conquest. The rise of Islam is a
success story no other religion
can match. Yet it was in Tunisia
that the Muslim warriors –

BACKGROUND

mujahidin – met their first serious resistance.

In AD 647 Abdallah ibn Saad's first incursion reached Sbeitla, where the patrician-bishop Gregory had defied Byzantium by declaring independence the previous year. A second Arab raid took place in 665 but only in 668–670 did 150,000 Muslims invade and stay. They founded Kairouan, which was to be their base for the conquest of the West, the later Arab capital (Carthage was ignored) and the religious centre in modern times.

There was mass conversion of the Berbers to Islam and many joined the Arab army. They

Tunisia's Roman sites in particular are amongst North Africa's most impressive

were, however, treated as second-class citizens, and consequent dissatisfaction led to their secession as Kharijites, Islamic 'outsiders'. Kharijite Berbers took Kairouan in 745 and were in and out of what little power there was until 800. An Arab governor named Ibrahim ibn el Aghlab then introduced what Tunisians consider to be their Golden Age. During their 109 years in power his descendants, the Aghlabites, built fortified medinas, *ribats* (monastery-barracks), great mosques and waterworks (of which only the pools at Kairouan remain). They also pacified the country, conquered Sicily in 827 and took back from Spain the idea of metal money.

In 909 the Aghlabites were evicted from Kairouan by the Fatimites, who transferred the capital to Mahdia. From here they quashed the still-belligerent Berbers and proceeded to conquer a Tunisian empire that stretched from Egypt in the east to the Atlantic in the west. They left this empire of *Ifriqia* in the hands of their allies the Zirites, who led the country through another artistic, commercial and agricultural heyday. In 1048 the Zirites repudiated the Fatimite caliphs in Cairo and gave their allegiance to the Sunnite regime in Baghdad, thus finally rejecting the unorthodox, Shi'ite beliefs of the Fatimites. They paid for it dearly. The Fatimite caliph el Mustansir, having on his hands two troublesome Arabian tribes, sent them westward.

There Beni Hilal and Sulaim wreaked havoc and some 1,700 years of progress was undone within a decade.

With the Berbers held in check, the Normans settled on Jerba in 1134. The Almohads, a Moroccan religious force, attacked Tunisia and the country became part of the Almohads' vast Mediterranean empire. After harassment of the Almohads from west and east, the Hafsite dynasty established itself in the new capital of Tunis in 1236. The expanding town became more cosmopolitan with allotted quarters for European envoys and merchants and Andalusian refugees from Spain.

● **Spanish** The Andalusians formed the skilled and civilised element of the population expelled from Spain. Their less-cultured compatriots were the Corsairs. Initially to take revenge on the Christian invaders, these seafarers turned to piracy. In 1520 Charles V of Spain became Holy Roman Emperor and France enlisted against him help from the Ottoman Turks. Tunisia became the scene of a confrontation between Muslim Turkey and Christian Spain, with the Corsair Barbarossa brothers playing a leading role. The Barbarossas, like their successor Dragut, were Muslim and backed by Turkey, so Charles V put to sea with 30,000 men and captured Tunis on 14 July 1535. In 1569 the Turkish Eulj Ali marched in from Algiers and retook the capital in 1574.

● **Turkish** By then all that was left of Spanish Tunisia was a series of impressive citadels along the coast. The Ottoman Turks, now ruling directly from Constantinople, imposed their standard pattern of provincial control. In 1587 Tunisia, Libya and Algeria each became a regency governed by a *pasha*. Junior officers (*deys*) mutinied in 1590 and one of their number, helped by the *bey*, rose to supreme power. Gradually the beys, the next tone down in the Turkish army scale, usurped it. In 1702 a dynasty was installed that, as the Husseinites, survived until 1957. On 27 July 1957 Tunisia's first independent parliament voted to abolish the monarchy.

French Intervention
In 1830 the French were installing themselves in Algeria and felt strong enough to frighten the bey next door into a treaty by which he renounced piracy. Inevitable bankruptcy made the regime dependent on long-term loans from French financiers, and gradually their stake in Tunisia's economy gave them a say in its government.

● **French** When in 1880 a Tunisian clan crossed the frontier into Algeria, the French felt entitled to rush in. They marched on Tunis and quelled by force the uprisings that broke out across the country. In 1881 and 1883, treaties obliged the bey to implement whatever reforms a French Resident Minister proposed, and French officials moved into all spheres of administration. Tunisia, technically only 'protected', was a thoroughgoing colony.

BACKGROUND

● **Allied and Axis** Though France collapsed at the start of World War II, many Tunisians volunteered to fight on the side of the Allies. The Allied landings in North Africa began on 8 November 1942. The Race for Tunis had started but was soon to be lost.

In 1943 the Germans advanced in a new offensive but the key towns of Beja, Mejez and Bou Arada stayed in Allied hands. In the south, Montgomery effectively overcame the Mareth Line in an operation almost as memorable as Hannibal's crossing of the Alps. The cornering of von Arnim's armies in the northeast made their resistance all the more intense, but their strongholds fell one by one and, on 13 May 1943, the Axis armies finally surrendered.

● **Tunisian** Nationalism was growing. Bourguiba, now acknowledged leader of the Destour Party, was forced to seek asylum, first in Egypt. The next decade was to see him alternately overseas and under arrest. As his influence, even from prison, succeeded in conciliating official thinking in Paris, so the intransigence of Tunisia's French colony increased.

Things had reached dire extremes when Bourguiba was permitted to return. His arrival at La Goulette on 1 June 1955 is celebrated annually as Victory Day, although it was not until the following year that Bourguiba seized the opportunity of a government change in France to negotiate independence.

Since the 1960s not only France again, but the USA, the UN, the World Bank, Germany, the Communist *bloc* and now the Arab oil states have all stepped in with aid to Tunisia.

The New Republic
Proclaimed on 25 July 1957, the new republic floundered through its first four years, meeting with French resistance. But for all that, Bourguiba increased his prestige internationally as the only head of a developing state to say 'boo' to de Gaulle, and to Nasser.

● **The Present** Tunisia is a republic, independent and headed by President Zine el Abidine Ben Ali. A former general, ambassador and prime minister, he succeeded Tunisia's first president, Habib Bourguiba, in a peaceful and constitutional deposition on 7 November 1987. It is Ben Ali's portrait that you see hanging everywhere.

The republic is divided into 23 *gouvernorats*, in which a *gouverneur* or *wali* is the president's right-hand man. The next step down in the administrative scale is the *délégation* or *mu'tamadia*; a governorate (*wilaya* in Arabic) consists of from three to 14; in each of the country's 199 delegations a *délégué* or *mu'tamad* represents the governor. Places such as Sousse, Monastir and Nabeul are *sièges* ('county-towns') of governorates of the same name in the immediate hinterland.

*The imposing Cathedral of
St Vincent de Paul, with gold
Christ and trumpeting angels*

TUNIS AND THE NORTH

TUNIS

With an out-of-town motorway,
cloverleaf flyovers and a *métro
léger* tramway, good hotels,
restaurants and nearby
beaches, modern stadiums and
excellent museums, a
population of more than a
million, a university older than
Oxford's, and even a well-
stocked zoo, Tunis is a
pleasantly pulsating place. And
within it lies a medieval town
which, with its close-packed
alleys of mosques, suqs, *zawias*
and ornate arched doorways,
belongs to another civilisation.
The **Place du 7 novembre 1987**,
with its clock tower, is the usual
coach drop-off/pick-up point
and where, if you come by car,
you can most conveniently
park. To the north the show-
piece Avenue Mohammed V
runs off between its lines of
palms to the Belvedere Park.
On the corner the upturned
pyramid of the Hôtel du Lac
looms over the **Ministry of
Tourism**, which offers free
brochures and information
about Tunisia.
Any tour of Tunis begins with
the main street ahead, named –
like every Tunisian main street
– **Avenue Habib Bourguiba**.
Precisely one mile (1.6km)
long, it runs from the edge of
the lake called El Bhira (the
Little Sea) almost to the medina
entrance known as the Bab el
Bahr (the Sea Gate). For the
salt waters of El Bhira once

covered this area right up to the walls of the medina. One Baroness Fasciotti, so the story goes, extended her lakeside property by paying the local dustmen to dump their cartloads in the shallows. This system, continued over the years, has resulted in the vast area which is now built upon between the medina and the still-retreating lake.

The blue skyscraper of the Africa Meridien Hotel, the grey-and-white monolith of the International Tunisia Hotel, the **Municipal Theatre** (a well-preserved period piece with a stucco façade of lyres, fronds and nudes) then, on the

The Rue Jamaa ez-Zitouna, main street of the medina

gardened **Place de l'Indépendance**, the vaguely bell-shaped statue (1978) of the philosopher-historian, Ibn Khaldun (1332–1406), forms a sightly but inconsequential link between the French Embassy (1862) and the **Cathedral of St Vincent de Paul** (1882). The Avenue Habib Bourguiba then narrows into the 'fashionable' Avenue de France, which is cut short by the Porte de France or **Bab el Bahr**, the watershed between the old and new Tunis. The Hafsites' walls have mostly been demolished and this 'Sea Gate' now stands isolated, unchanged since 1848 until it received, in 1985, the fine restoration it both needed and deserved. The **British Embassy** occupies a historic building, the most prominent on this Place de la Victoire. Along right, the Rue des Glacières turns into the **Rue Zarkoun**, Tunis' equivalent of London's street markets in Portobello Road and Petticoat Lane.

◆◆◆ TUNIS MEDINA ✓

In Tunis is both the largest and best-maintained example of the medinas seen also in Hammamet, Kairouan, Sfax, Sousse, Monastir and Mahdia. The word in Arabic means nothing more than 'town' (French-speaking Tunisians prefer in fact '*la Ville arabe*') – the once high-walled, still narrow-alleyed burghs that medieval travellers hurried to reach before the massive gate (the *bab*) closed safe against

intruders for the night.
The spirit of Tunis' Medina is unique – it seems not only detached from the modern capital but detached from time itself. Perhaps the best way to imbibe the spirit of the place is to wander up past the Great Mosque and around the suqs at random. Alternatively you may prefer to follow the itinerary below, starting and finishing at the Bab el Bahr or 'Sea Gate'. Behind the Bab el Bahr the **Rue Jamaa ez-Zitouna** climbs between open-front shops which, if the suqs (or souks) were still named after their trades as once they were, would make this the Suq of Souvenirs. Asking-prices are arbitrary, so barter.
A first arcade is partly antiquarian, the second gives on to the **Great Mosque**. The Jami' ez-Zituna (the Mosque of the Olive-tree) is the largest and oldest in Tunis, and second in Tunisia only to Kairouan's. It was started by the Umayyad rulers in 732, completed by the Aghlabites in 864, enlarged by the Zirites in the 10th century and again by the Turks in 1637. The ceiling was replaced in 1782 and the whole structure restored between 1962 and 1975. You enter from the imposing eastern gallery. The visit is permitted weekdays from 09.30 to 12.00hrs and 14.00 to 16.30hrs, but only as far as the patio and courtyard. Now begins the most picturesque quarter. This central complex of high-vaulted suqs, each specialising originally in one trade, was

mostly built by the 13th-century Hafsites and rebuilt by the 18th-century beys. Turn right along the Great Mosque's façade and left into a beautiful suq.

The Perfumers
The 13th-century **Souk el Attarine**, the Perfumers – narrow, low shops all green and gold, selling henna and sundry herbs for perfumes; the ceilings stalactitic with pink, white, blue, gold or plain candles, some even worked in silver, and the shelves amber, orange and pink with jars of incense and heavy perfumes.

Then loop left along the 14th-century **Souk des Étoffes** (the Cloth Market). This runs into the **Souk des Femmes** (Women) but turn right by the tiled fountain of the Bab es-Shefa and climb the narrow **Souk el Leffa**. At no 58 is the tourist supermarket where a small tip will get you up the back stairs – past the vast gilt-and-mirror 'bed of the bey' – to the so-called Palais d'Orient. As an Oriental Palace it is phoney – the tiled arches and walls are a recent setting for the older fragments of masonry – but it was the first of the several tourist *terrasses* and offers a fine topside view of the city's skyline. Opposite, downhill, is the Souk el Kebabjia (Silks) and, inches uphill, the **Souk el Berka**. This, one of the loveliest, has an ugly past. Amidst the shop-fronts in their pretty pastel mauves and pinks, reds, soft greens and golds, stands the

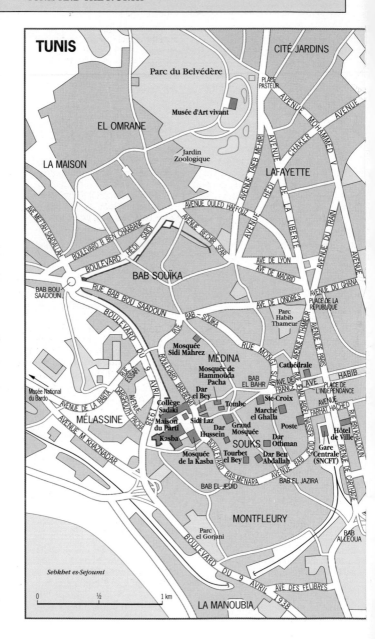

former Slave Market. Red-and-green pillars, mural tiles and jewellers are all you see now of the place where women and children, Christian and often English, were once put up for auction.

From the Berka's far end the **Souk et-Trouk** runs down right to rejoin the **Souk el Attarine**. Yusef Dey designed this vaulted 'Suq of the Turks' in 1630 as the city's finest thoroughfare; its reputation amongst visitors today centres on the **M'rabet**. Its namesakes – three marabouts interred to one side - awe the lofty, solemn café; the upstairs Restaurant d'Ommok Sannafa is noisier nightly with Arab musicians and an oriental floorshow.

Turn beneath the Great Mosque's four-square minaret, which was raised to its present 145 feet (44m) in 1896. The **Rue Sidi Ben Arous** is flanked by the **Mosque of Hamuda Pasha** (Mosquée de Hammoûda Pacha). A model mosque in every sense, its design is copied in the Bourguiba Mosque in Monastir, and it is fashionable to have your marriage or a son's circumcision solemnised by prayer here. Steps lead into the courtyard with the elegant octagonal minaret and Hamuda Pasha's *tourbet* (also from 1655). Turn right down the **Rue de la Kasba**, right into the Rue el Jeloud and right again up the Impasse Echemmahia. At no 9 you will (for a small tip) be welcomed up the stairs and along the alley to the **Tomb of Princess Aziza Othmana**. It occupies the Medersat

The elegant Mosque of Hamuda Pasha, Tunis Medina

Echemmahia, built in the 13th century and rebuilt in 1647. Othman Dey's daughter Fatima, who died the year before, may have been famous for her charity – whence *Aziza*, 'Beloved' – but the two ornate *qubbas* of 24 tombs (hers on the right between the bedrolls and the bicycles) have been rather parsimoniously restored. Opposite the cul-de-sac, the **Souk el Blagjia** (1757) descends, left, between some shoe-shops to the Rue de la Kasba, which winds on down, right, to the Bab el Bhar.

Accommodation

Catering more for visiting officials and company accounts than tourists, Tunis' best hotels are markedly costlier than those in the resorts. The **Africa Meridien**, 4-star luxe (tel: 01 347 477), and the **International Tunisia**, 4-star luxe (tel: 01 254 855), are very central on the main avenue; the **Abou Nawas**, 4-star luxe (tel: 01 350 355), is the newest in this class, and the **Tunis Hilton**, 4-star luxe (tel: 01 282 000), is quieter out of town, with magnificent views (and admirable security) from its hilltop sloped with lawns and gardens. Friendliest of the normal 4-star establishments is the **Belvédère**, (tel: 01 783 133), in the embassy and better-business district of the same name – round the corner from the **Diplomat**, 4-star (tel: 01 785 233), and a short walk from the bustling **El Mechtel**, 4-star (tel: 01 783 200). The **Ambassadeurs**, 3-star (tel: 01 288 011), is in the same district, the **Ibn Khaldoun**, 3-star (tel: 01 783 211), nearer to the airport, more central and enterprising; the **Majestic**, 3-star (tel: 01 242 848), is a fading French-colonial period piece, the **Golf Royal**, 3-star (tel: 01 344 311), newer and brassy, and the **Hôtel du Lac**, 3-star (tel: 01 258 322), an architectural oddity. Cheaper hotels cluster in side-streets off Avenue Bourguiba.

◆◆◆
CARTHAGE

Once the capital of a whole empire whose mariners sailed to the ends of the then-known world, Carthage is nowadays an up-market commuters' garden-suburb.
To prevent the site's archaeological treasures being further built on or carried off,

UNESCO in 1972 launched an 'unprecedented rescue operation' to safeguard Carthage. For ten years teams of archaeologists from Britain, North America and several European states worked alongside Tunisians to excavate and document the few remaining undeveloped plots. Opposite the TGM station Salammbo (and closest to Tunis), the **tophet** (crematorium) is signposted '*Sanctuaire punique*'. Here stood the temples of Tanit and Baal Hammon who demanded human sacrifice. To the right, surrounded by overgrown gardens, gape the ugly pits where the children's ashes were discovered in 1921 (and exhumed in 1942–3).

Atrocities
So many 4–12-year-olds were strangled, then burned, in the course of 600 years that the urns filled the allotted area; fresh layers of urns and stelae were therefore laid on top.

Stelae are the commemorative headstones, varying in style through the centuries, that now crowd the area to the left. Follow the Rue Hannibal on from the Tophet and the **Port Punique (Punic Ports)** lie to the right and ahead. The nearer of these now placid village ponds was the mercantile port, the more northerly a larger *cothon* for the Punic navy. With its colonnaded dry docks for 220 vessels, the latter was the pride of Carthage's sea-power.

Continuing along the main road after the appropriately Punic start, your move into Roman Carthage should begin with the Roman and Palaeo-Christian **Museum**.

A dog's leg across the main Avenue Bourguiba, the Rue Ibn Chabbat runs down to the seafront restaurant and the Punic site known as the **Quartier Magon**.

From the Shell and Esso cross-roads ahead, the Avenue des Thermes d'Antoniose squeezes between coaches and souvenir sellers to the **Thermes d'Antonin Pius (Baths of Antoninus Pius)**. Lying northwest/southeast along the shore, the 9 acres (3.6ha) of masonry impress: but what astonishes here is the realisation that most of this is merely the basement, the 'works' of the baths, with stores of wood for the furnaces and earthenware pipes for the hot water they supplied. The actual baths – one part for women, one for men – were on an upper floor, level with the present boundary track; their ceiling was supported by 12 fluted and grey granite columns, and one Corinthian capital alone has been found weighing some four tons. (It now crowns the 'grand column' resurrected in the baths.) The building of the 'Imperial Baths' was started by the emperor Hadrian (AD 117–38) and completed by his successor Antoninus Pius (138–61). Turn inland again and uphill, across the Shell and Esso cross-roads. To the right is the **Parque Archéologique des Villas Romaines (Archaeological Park** of **Roman Villas**) – an evocative hillside of high Roman house-walls, cisterns, columns and capitals, steep well-paved streets and the Antiquarium. The next sight, right of the Avenue du 7 novembre, is the **Théâtre d'Hadrian (Hadrian's theatre)**. Although fine Roman statuary has been discovered here, both Tunisians and foreign residents now know the theatre best for its July–August festival of classical and jazz concerts, classical plays and ballet. The broad avenue then reaches

the low crest by the **Thermes de Gargilius (Baths of Gargilius)**. Worked by Americans in the early 1920s, the baths became famous in early church history as the site of the Council of Carthage where (in 411) 565 bishops attempted to end the rift between the Catholics and the Donatist sect. At the foot of the hill beyond, the 15 **Cisternes de la Malga (Cisterns of La Malga)** are reached by a narrow cactus track. To the left is the **Amphithéâtre des Martyrs (Martyrs' Amphitheatre)**.

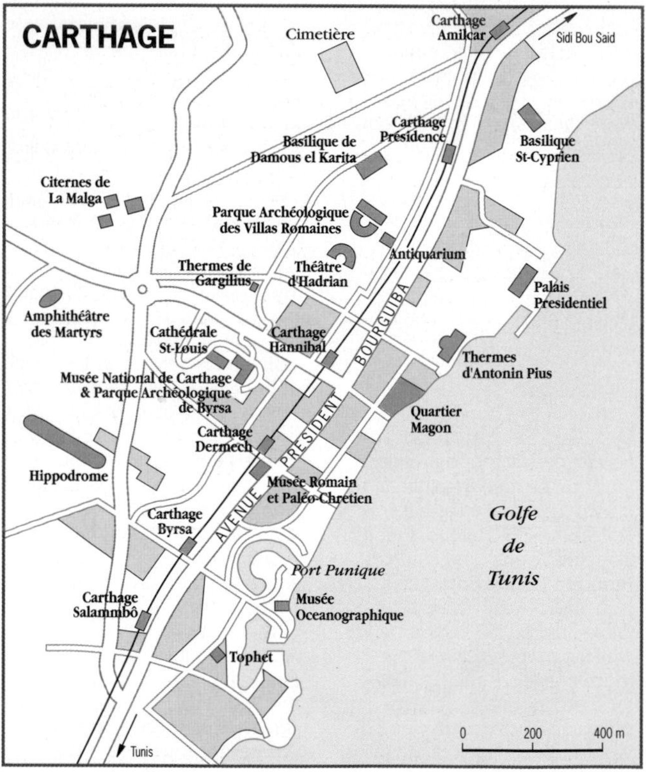

CARTHAGE

Cimetière

Carthage Amilcar

Sidi Bou Said

Carthage Présidence

Basilique de Damous el Karita

Basilique St-Cyprien

Citernes de La Malga

Parque Archéologique des Villas Romaines

Antiquarium

Thermes de Gargilius

Théâtre d'Hadrian

BOURGUIBA

Palais Présidentiel

Amphithéâtre des Martyrs

Cathédrale St-Louis

Carthage Hannibal

Thermes d'Antonin Pius

Musée National de Carthage & Parque Archéologique de Byrsa

PRESIDENT

Carthage Dermech

Quartier Magon

Hippodrome

Musée Romain et Paléo-Chrétien

AVENUE

Golfe de Tunis

Carthage Byrsa

Port Punique

Carthage Salammbô

Musée Oceanographique

Tophet

Tunis

0   200   400 m

Cardinal Lavigerie erected the column and installed in the vaults below a chapel to the memory of St Perpetua, most famous of the Christians thrown to the animals near by at the orders of a fellow 'African', the emperor Septimius. Conspicuous on the hilltop behind stands the brash *nouveau riche* of bourgeois Carthage. It is customary to be rude about the Gothic façade, Romanesque proportions and spire-surrounded dome of the **Cathedral of St Louis**, but it has appeal. It was built in 1884–90 as the cathedral of the 'Revived Diocese of Africa'.

To the south of the cathedral extends a steep hillside, the **Parque Archéologique de Byrsa (Archaeological Park of Byrsa)**, on which Punic masonry and Roman walling seemed puzzlingly overlapped. The archaeological riddle was solved by the French UNESCO team, whose excavations led to the significant discovery that Rome not only razed the Punic capital but also physically removed the temple area that crowned it.

The site also serves as thoroughfare to the **Musée National de Carthage (National Museum of Carthage)**, right next to the White Fathers' ex-headquarters. The museum now housed in a new building has a fine collection of Roman and Christian mosaics, statues and stelae, striking Phoenician sculptures, funerary masks and casks, a case of antique ladies' make-up, plaques in Punic script and two splendid sarcophagi depicting their 4th-century BC incumbents. Plus a painting by a highly imaginative White Father of a sumptuous Roman palace. (Archaeologists differ on whether in fact a 4th-century proconsul's palace actually occupied this site.)

The road skirts the cathedral, hairpins past the Reine Didon Hotel, and winds down most of Byrsa's 205 feet (62m): left to the Tunis–La Marsa road, right to the Hannibal TGM station and from there back to the Shell and Esso cross-roads.

Access
Carthage's scattered and isolated features are best reached by car (9 miles/15km from Tunis), but if you have more time than money to spend, a very pleasant alternative is to take the TGM-tramway from Tunis Marine station. At the Carthage–Hannibal station stand *hippomobiles* (horse-carriages), which will trundle you round the principal sites in a leisurely, Edwardian way. You can either agree on the price in advance or disagree afterwards.

Accommodation
Good at the **Reine Elyssa Didon**, Rue Mendes France, 3-star (tel: 01 275 447), with meals magnificent in its scenic 'Punic' restaurant, homely in the **Résidence Carthage**, 6 Rue Hannibal Salammbô, 2-star (tel: 01 731 072) and panoramic but package in the **Amilcar**, 3-star (tel: 01 740 788).

Shopping
Shopping is for books on Carthage and Rome (best at the Antonin Shop opposite the Baths of Antoninus Pius) and for

phoney Roman 'finds'. (*Caveat emptor* – 'buyer beware' – of the 'Roman oil-lamps' everywhere: had the ancients really left behind all the lamps you see for sale, they must have used them much as we do matches.)

◆◆◆
SIDI BOU SAID ✓

If your brochures show a 'typical Tunisian village' of cobbled streets, white walls, blue studded doors and black mashrabias, it will probably be 'Sidi Bou'. This picturesque village winds round the top of a hill which became a beacon for early navigators and a haven for this century's artists, writers and affluent gentlefolk. A Muslim legend has it that St Louis did not die on Byrsa Hill but took French leave of his army, married a Berber girl and became the local saint Bou Said (known for curing rheumatism and stopping scorpions from stinging). However, St Louis did not arrive until 1270 and the historical Abu Said Khalifa bin Yahia et-Temimi el Baji died in 1231.

Today's influx of Westerners, whether trippers or settlers, is something of a historical irony. Atop the ancient Cap Carthage, where the Punic suburb of Megara spread, Muslims of the Middle Ages built a *ribat* (fortress) from which to defend the coast against Christian raiders; St Louis died in the shadow of this stronghold of early Sufism, Islamic mysticism; the Corsairs made 'Sidi Bou' their mascot, the patron saint of anti-Christian piracy, and although Charles V, from 1535 to

Despite one and a half centuries of attracting tourists, Sidi Bou Said has retained great charm

1574 maintained a Spanish garrison here (which included Cervantes, pre-*Don Quixote*), Christians were actually forbidden to enter the village until 1820.

Whether Muslim or not, you may now wander unrestricted: up from the car park, past the 'museum' (in fact the municipal gallery with regular art exhibitions) then to the much-vaunted **Café des Nattes** for your almost mandatory cup of mint tea on the mat-covered seats; then along past the shop selling sticky *bambaloni* cakes and the Shrine of Sidi Bou Said, once a sanctuary for criminals. Of the village's many sumptuous mansions only two are frankly public: the **Dar Said**, a 'honeymoon hotel', and the **Dar Zarrouk** with its panoramic terrace restaurant. Coach parties are usually shown the same panorama free, from the screen of eucalyptus that overlooks the gulf and Bou Kornine.

Accommodation

The **Sidi Bou Said Hotel**, 4-star (tel: 01 740 411), an adjunct of the Sidi Dhrif school of hotel management, is government-run (so your fellow guests will range from OAU officials to pan-African athletes).

◆◆
LA MARSA

Though its name means 'the Port' (something it never had), La Marsa's role is as a summer residence, formerly of the beys, nowadays of Tunis' better-off. The spacious main street forks right by the post office and turns by the French ambassador's residence into the *corniche*, a palm-lined promenade. The rest of old seafront La Marsa is stucco-fronted and shuttered French beach-homes alongside fly-by-night *crêperies*. Both thrive on the *sayafa*, the summer-month renters from Tunis who quintuple the township's year-round population of 38,000 souls. Inland, behind the rebuilt arcades of shops, lies the Saf-Saf Square with the originally Hafsite mosque and the **Café Saf-Saf**, built round and taking its name from the white poplar trees. The café boasts a courtyard well, supposedly

Hafsite, from which water is raised by a blinkered camel turning small circles all day. The beys held their summer court at La Marsa, though there is no visible sign of the dwarfs, or the eunuchs, that still in the 1960s were supposed to survive here from their retinues. Palaces remain: like the **Abdulaya**, the monumental hulk behind the post office (left of the road to Gammarth), and the British ambassador's residence (left of the road to Tunis, half a mile/1km out).

GAMMARTH

Smart Gammarth vies with Carthage as suavest of the 'Tunis North' resorts. From La Marsa, the fork signposted 'Hauts de Gammarth' climbs to the **French military cemetery**, in which 4,010 killed in World War II lie in semicircular ranks along the slopes of Jebel Khawi, the Hollow Mountain (because of the cavities of an early Hebrew necropolis). The lower cliff road – 'Bord de Mer' – serves a hillside of hotels and highly desirable homes: past the beautiful Abou Nawas and the Megara hotels and down past the rebuilt Tour Blanche Hotel to the 'Sinbad', Les Ombrelles and Les Dunes restaurants. As the cliffs, sandstone and deeply eroded, crowd out the beach, the road climbs a hill yellow with spring mimosa to a crest on which the ruins of Ben Ayed are now hard-pressed by the Saudi-financed, but apparently abandoned villa-complex called 'Les Jardins de

Carthage'. Then down past the Beau Geste edifice of the aborted Grand Hôtel du Casino and on to the Baie des Singes Hotel and the restaurants Le Pêcheur and Les Coquillages. A war-time bunker and the Restaurant La Vague next picket a beach invaded by local car-loads every summer. The road no longer peters out into beach but culminates in the Cap Carthage Méditerranée project.

Accommodation
Superb in the **Abou Nawas**, Avenue Taïeb Mehriri, 4-star luxe (tel: 01 741 444). Below it in standing come the **Megara**, Avenue Taïeb Mehriri, 3-star (tel: 01 740 366), and the **Tour Blanche**, Avenue Taïeb Mehirir, unclassified, (tel: 01 271 694). The Cap Carthage cluster consists of the **Cap Carthage Hotel**, Chott El Ghaba, 3-star (tel: 01 740 064, its 'Masters Restaurant' a token of its preoccupation with tennis), the **Molka**, Raoued, La Marsa, 3-star (tel: 01 740 242), and the rather far-flung **Dar Naouar** holiday village (tel: 01 741 000).

Restaurants
Excellent in this fashionable garden suburb, reasonably priced (but packed in summer): on the beach of Sidi Abdul-Aziz outside La Marsa, the **Restaurant Le Golfe**; in a dip of the main road beyond the Tour Blanche Hotel, the **Sinbad**, **Les Ombrelles** and **Les Dunes**; and on the beach beyond the cliffs, the restaurants **Le Pêcheur** (the

National Fisheries Offices, and recommended), **Les Coquillages** ('Shellfish', self-explanatory) and **La Vague** ('The Wave').

◆
BORJ CEDRIA
Now a sprawling satellite settlement, this halt on the old main road south was for years little more than a rail junction for the defunct Cap Bon line and the roadside Relais des Coupoles, a restaurant in super-Tunisian style (but designed by a Bulgarian in 1967). Its neighbour has been the **German military cemetery**

A superb selection of local crafts is on offer in Sidi Bou Said, as in the rest of Tunisia. Woodwork is an excellent buy

since 1975. Borj Cedria owes its place on the tourist map to the best beach within easy reach of Tunis, and the three hotels built on it.

Accommodation

Fair in the family-run **Salwa**, 3-star (tel: 01 290 830), massively French-package in the **Dar**, 2-star (tel: 01 290 188) and unpredictable as yet in the **Medisea**, 3-star (tel: 01 293 013).

◆◆◆
MUSÉE NATIONAL DU BARDO (BARDO NATIONAL MUSEUM) ✓

Le Bardo

With probably the world's best display of mosaics and certainly

North Africa's best Roman collection, the museum is well worth the short sortie from Tunis.

After the archaeological shop come chambers of Punic stelae and earthenware from the *tophets* (crematoria) of Carthage and Sousse (8th–2nd centuries BC), with a (usually locked) side-room of Punic treasures. The Punic Rooms lead back to the entrance hall (two remarkably preserved Punic sarcophagi in wood complete with contents). Beyond the stairs of the ceramic-tiled Arab Palace lies the Corridor of Stelae and Sarcophagi (these and marble funerary statues, plus the toilet). To the left the corridor leads to an attractive Palaeo-Christian Room with font, tomb covers and mosaics of less sophistication but more impact: Daniel in the lions' den, builders at work and the Christian hallmarks of doves, grapes, labarum-signs and Dog Latin. Off this is the Bulla Regia Room, with massive statues of gods and emperors it must have been a joy to unearth. The broad staircase up from the Christian Room is flanked by mosaics, many from Tabarka. Turn left by the Apollo at the top and the sight is unexpectedly beautiful after the businesslike ground floor. The upper patio of the palace – grilled windows, colonnades, galleries, pendant arches and a ceiling almost Baroque in pink, green and gilt – now houses a magnificent array of antiquity.

Across the patio from the

entrance lies the former Music Room, with galleries and painted-wood ceiling – again delightful, although the mosaics may perhaps begin to pall. The dais at the end of the patio gives on to a perfect Tunisian chamber of tiled walls and sculpted-plaster cupolas, in which stands the famous 3rd-century mosaic of Virgil and the muses Clio and Melpomene (from Sousse), and adjoining which is the Prehistoric Room (flints, photographs and 'the world's first known monument of religious inspiration' …a pile of stones).

Far right come the Mahdia Rooms. About 81 BC a whole galley-load of Grecian treasures sank in a storm three miles (5km) off Mahdia. The wooden ship rotted but its bronze and stone cargo, half buried in the sea-bed, was luckily spotted by a sponge-diver in 1907. It took until 1913 to raise this unique treasure trove – from 1,500lb (680kg) anchors to bronze bed fittings and dwarf and hermaphrodite miniatures, from barnacle pock-marked capitals to shapely urns.

The stairs to the next floor take you up between walls tapestried with mosaics. In the near corner, room after room is floored and walled with mosaics depicting contemporary beasts and beliefs, and graphically – often heroically – recording Roman tastes, activities and lifestyles. Beneath the gilded arches of this upper gallery, cases display lamps, stamps and seals: statues and brooches in bronze: vessels exquisite in iridescent glass, and vases, masks, moulds, jugs, busts and statuettes in terracotta.

Open: Tuesday to Sunday 09.30–16.30hrs.
Closed: Mondays.

Access

By bus from Tunis – no 3 from the Place du 7 novembre 1987, the Avenue Habib Bourguiba or the Avenue de Paris.

◆
UTICA (UTIQUE)

The history of *Outih*, the first known Phoenician settlement in Tunisia, provides in many ways a counterpoint to that of Carthage. Utica was founded by trader-sailors from Tyre on a prehistoric site in 1101 BC (according to Pliny the Elder). Thus Carthage's senior by some 300 years, the northern city maintained its independence of the Punic capital for a further 300 years, being forced into allegiance in the 5th century BC. Agathocles, who failed to take Carthage, captured Utica in 308 BC. After the First Punic War, the rebel mercenaries found refuge here, and Hamilcar Barca's consequent reduction of Utica was curiously avenged in the Third Punic War, when it not only refused to assist Carthage but even served as Rome's operational base against the sister-city – thereby escaping the fate that Scipio inflicted on the capital and its allies, Punic Bizerta, Kelibia and Nabeul. As a further Roman 'reward', Utica was made first a free city, in 144

BC, then capital of the *Provincia Africa*. Marius landed here with his legions to put down Jugurtha in 107 BC, and in 49–45 BC the Pompeian resistance to Caesar in Africa was maintained by 'Cato of Utica'. Great-grandson of the Cato who so famously inveighed against Carthage, he stabbed himself, at Utica, after Caesar's final triumph at Thapsus. Though Utica continued to prosper in the 2nd and 3rd centuries AD, it was probably – and ironically – this Pompeian association that prompted Caesar to have Carthage resurrected.

None of which can be seen or even conjectured from the present-day remains.

Half of Utica's interest is the **Antiquarium**: to the left of the approach-road, before the site, this renovated museum stands between a venerable rubber-tree and a displaced mosaic (a splendid head of Neptune in a two-dimensional aquarium). Its contents are Punic stelae and a sarcophagus complete with equipment (the Carthaginians believed you needed household gear in the hereafter), Grecian pottery and statues, Roman busts and ladies' toiletry, a Thelwell horse in terracotta and the usual amphorae, coins and oil-lamps.

Found a few yards further on, the site was excavated first in 1905 but mostly in 1946–58. Of the various edifices identified by their main features – the 'House of the Treasure', 'of the Hunt', 'of the Capitals' – only the **House of the Fountain** is of any great interest: an arch with neat sockets for the roof-beams and bolts; three boarded, and well-preserved mosaics which the gardener-watchman uncovers to reveal scenes of fishermen and fish; rooms off with mosaic and marble floors in pink, green, cream and grey, and the lead piping broken illustratively open in places.

◆

GHAR EL MELH

Known locally as 'Unq el Jemel' ('the Camel's neck') and

Fish still swim in the mosaics of the House of the Fountain, Utica

formerly as 'Porto Farina', this pretty fishing-port has an interesting history and a fertile hinterland. The name of *Rusucmona* is all that remains of this original outpost of Punic Utica.

After the Roman period came 1,200 years of historical somnolence, rudely cut short first by the emperor Charles V, who sheltered and watered his fleet here before raiding La Goulette, and by Admiral Blake, who bombarded the port in 1654 when Hamuda Pasha refused to release English captives. In 1837 Ahmed Bey began a grandiose project of palaces and barracks in this port the Corsairs had made famous. The three fortresses they built became prisons; only in 1965 were the last of the inmates transferred to Bizerta. Today, with the 12-square-mile

Ghar el Melh ('cave of salt'), a picturesque fishing port with a long past, now rarely visited

(31sq km) anchorage ruined by the River Mejerda's silt, Ghar el Melh is known for its potatoes – and its veiled women.

The road in winds its way through tight market-gardens and past the first fort, complete with its massive bastions and an impressive moat. (Ghazi Sultan Mohammed is honoured as its builder in the dedicatory plaque.) The road narrows through an arcade of booths, passing the Martyrs' Memorial and the simple mosque on the left and the second fortress/prison/college on the right. You veer past the third ex-prison down to the abandoned shipsheds and battlemented mole of the photogenic port.

◆
BIZERTA (BIZERTE)
This northern port/resort has as its 'hinterland' the 43-square-mile (111sq km) Lake of Bizerta, a natural harbour that first attracted the Phoenician sailors to found *Hippo Diarrhytus* here and finally made the French so reluctant to leave. Your first sight of the lake betokens its present importance: the oyster- and mussel beds of the National Fisheries Office. Until 1963 the French were in jealous possession of this former Corsair haven; the *risorgimento* feared it as 'a pistol levelled at the heart of Italy'; it was a key operational base, bitterly contested, of World War II, and the first NATO generals considered it vital to Western defence. Nuclear thinking, supertankers and a closed Suez Canal made Bizerta redundant.

The road from Tunis crosses the 328-yard (300m) **swing bridge** and lands you plumb in the centre of the checkerboard French-protectorate town. The **Avenue du Président Habib Bourguiba** skirts the Martyrs' Square, tips one gardened side of the Old Port and ends in Bizerta's 'esplanade': government offices and the **Sport-Nautique bar-restaurant** and, round the corner, the police station, bus station and Regional Tourist Office.

The photogenic **Old Port** separates the new town from the old. It is difficult to imagine how, until 1890, the Old Port was part of the original canal through to the lake. In the canal was an island, since re-attached to become the quay on which now stands the **ONA store** (with a customarily tasteful display). Opposite, across the Place Lahedire Bouchoucha, the quaint fountain was supposedly erected, and inscribed in Turkish and Arabic, by Yusef Dey in 1642. To the right you pass another inscribed fountain and turn left to the Place du Marché. Here you enter the **kasba** by a vaulted passage, bent to hamper medieval invaders. The 17th-century Mosque of the Medina confronts you, its minaret retiled but its interest minimal. Across the Place du Marché from the kasba gate, the Rue des Armuriers runs past the plain mosque and *tourbet* of Sidi Mustari and, through the arch, the Ironworkers' Suq. After the 17th-century **Great Mosque** ('Visitors are Invited to put on Correct Dress and not Smoking') the alley winds less interestingly through a quarter of discreet shops, white-arched lanes and black-veiled women to Bab el Jedid, 'Newgate'. The hilltop behind is picturesquely crowned by the **Fort of Spain**, where the bastioned walls converge. Also known as the Fort of Sidi Salem, the citadel was built by the Turks in 1573 and reworked by Yusef Dey in 1620–42, to be transformed in 1968 into a starkly attractive open-air theatre.

Accommodation
The **Corniche**, 3-star (tel: 02 31 844), is comfortable. Its good beach is shared by the **Nador**,

2-star (tel: 02 31 848), the **Jalta**, (tel: 02 32 250), and the holiday-campish **El-Kebir** (tel: 02 31 892). Further westward, the **Petit Mousse**, 2-star (tel: 02 32 185), has a reputed restaurant but no pool, the **El Khayem** terminates the last stretch of beach (tel: 02 32 120), while the **Sidi Salem** survives nearer the port (tel: 02 32 126).

◆◆
TABARKA

The mountains of Khroumiria step back from the golden beaches to leave room for this compact town. The sands stretch round a sheltered bay, giving way in places to rocky promontories. A pretty island-cone offshore is topped by a castle to complete the picturesque scene.
At present, the ambitious Montazah-Tabarka development project, funded in large part by Saudi Arabia, is under way: a marina around the fishing-port; hotels and 'Moorish' villas along the westward cliffs of Larmel, and on the Morjane hills and beaches to the east.
If Tabarka has waited 2,000 years for its promotion from port to resort, there is good historical reason. After Carthage the Phoenicians founded *Thabraca* (Bushy Place) and the subsequent Roman port handled not only 'Numidian' marble from Chemtou but also the cork, leather, timber and minerals of Khroumiria. The town's Christian connections we know from the mosaics in the Bardo

Museum. Its coral attracted the Genoese families of Lomellini and Grimaldi who, the story goes, had Charles V swap the captured Corsair Dragut for the island of *Tabarque* in 1542. As a Christian outpost the island numbered some 1,200 inhabitants when, in 1741, Ali Pasha Bey cut short the Franco-Italian wrangle over who owned Tabarka by sending his son to take it and sell them as slaves. Razing the 'imposing ruins of an immense edifice' – the Roman baths – in order to build the town square, burying Punic and Roman remains beneath their styleless streets, the French 'urbanised' in the 1900s. Blissfully ignorant of this archaeological sacrilege, their young compatriots now contribute most to Tabarka's summer popularity.
From the Hôtel de France in the main street, a quarter-mile (½km) cul-de-sac runs past the vestigial Roman vaults by the Fisheries Office to the **Aiguilles** ('Needles') – 60-foot (18m) stacks, fantastically eroded.
To the left of the hotel, the Café Andalous has a cluttered but fascinating décor of antique and oriental bric-à-brac. The corner opposite, across the Rue du Peuple, was planned as an archaeological workshop. Its sponsors happily dropped the project when, digging the foundations, they discovered (only 8 inches/20cm below the French tarmac) Roman roads, house-walls, pottery and coins from the 1st century AD.
Opposite, the **basilica**, a former church converted from a Roman cistern, acts as a

backdrop to the open-air theatre of the annual **Festival de Tabarka**. From the main street, plain roads run down to the beach. The **island** dominates everything, 1,968 feet (600m) long, 1,312 feet (400m) wide and 229 feet (70m) high. The French attached it with a 1,312-foot (400m) mole in 1952 and a leisurely track winds up to the Genoese fort and the lighthouse.

Accommodation
Dignified in the 'French manorial' **Mimosas**, 3-star (tel: 08 43 028), picturesque above the town but far from the

One of the remarkable mosaics which have survived in the Roman city of Bulla Regia

beach, or more determinedly sporty in the **Tabarka Club El Morjane**, 3-star (tel: 08 44 453).

Shopping
For coral (most of Tunisia's being landed on this coast), for planters of cork-oak (from the forests of the hinterland) and for the quaint terracotta objects made in nearby Sejenane: buff platters, jugs and statuettes patterned in maroon and black.

◆
AIN DRAHAM
This Khroumir mountain village, 15 steep miles (24km) from Tabarka, nestles close to the Algerian frontier, its Arabic name meaning 'Spring of Money'. Tunisian brochures tend to overdo it – for them it has rarity value. It is reminiscent of Switzerland, with cottages white-walled and red-roofed, oak-trees on the slopes and sleek cows in the fields, wood-and-gloom Alpine hotels, walks through the slatted sunlight of forest in summer, hunting the wild boar in winter. The village consists of housing and administration blocks above the single main street and, opposite the Beau Séjour Hotel, a shop selling *la Céramique khroumirienne*: glossy objects local but neither ethnic nor aesthetic.

Accommodation/Restaurants
Possible in the **Beau Séjour** (tel: 08 47 005), passable at **Les Chênes**, 4 miles (7km) further, 2-star (tel: 08 47 211), but preferable at the **Rihana**, 2-star (tel: 08 47 391/2).

BULLA REGIA

The distinctive feature of the ruins of this magnificent Roman city are its palatial underground villas with many fine mosaics *in situ*. It is open 08.30–17.30hrs (winter); 07.00–19.00hrs (summer).

The entrance to the main site lies beside the road, opposite what was a café and may one day be a museum. The **Baths of Julia Memmia** confront you, a 2nd-century complex excavated partly in 1909–24 with impressive mosaics, arches and high-vaulted walls, intact or restored, in the main halls and side-rooms. You enter via chambers in which the tapered tubes used to shape the quick-drying plaster are still visible in the vaulting. Leave through the fine northwest façade, where stairs climb to a well-paved road. Opposite, the track uphill becomes a paved Roman lane climbing first to the **House of the Peacock** – each edifice is named from the finest mosaic found in it – and the **House of the Hunt**, recognisable by its reddish columns. This 'Maison de la Chasse' is the best of Bulla's subterranean mansions: a colonnade surrounds the *atrium* (courtyard) and, in the rooms off, there are mosaics on the platforms raised for beds. Take the paved Roman lane along the 'top' of this palace to the neighbouring complex of walls, stumpy columns and fine fish-and-fowl mosaics – a temple to judge by the mosaic inscription *hecdomvsdei*, 'This (is) the House of God'. Next

(east again) comes the **Fishing House**, the street-level area of which is an astonishing complex of rock-rimmed vents for the ducts that descend to the less elaborate *atrium* and 'cloister' rooms below.

On the paved lane running north alongside this 'Maison de la Pêche', the first intact mosaic floor indicates the so-called **House of Amphitrite**: her head an exquisite mosaic on a background of black tesserae and, in the main *triclinium*, the same face on a nude body astride a creature without a head but with wings for forelegs and hind-legs back-to-front. Descend again to the Fishing House and climb the well-trodden bank to the track down past the installations of nearby Jendouba's water-supply. The **Temple of Apollo**, Bulla's patron, lies left of the grassy **forum**, from which steps continue down to the market area. The clover-leaf bath here, beautiful with mosaic, was reserved for the actors of the **theatre** ahead. Similar to Dougga's – save that here, as at Kasserine, many balustrades remain in place – it is equally evocative.

A well-paved lane then leads west between the Temple of Isis and an unusual Roman feature: two long public esplanades with ornamental 'moats'; and so to the exit.

Access

Inaccessible by public transport. Best visited from Jendouba (6 miles/9km), Aïn Draham (23 miles/37km) or Tabarka (38 miles/62km).

HAMMAMET, CAP BON, THE WESTERN SITES

◆◆◆

HAMMAMET

Thanks to exquisite beaches and colourful gardens set along two gentle bays, this otherwise ordinary fishing-village vies with Sousse as Tunisia's leading resort.

It is easy to see why hoteliers followed the foreign artists and aesthetes who settled here in the 1920s. And why the Romans preceded them *en masse*. From the *colonia* promoted in AD 179 by a local proconsul, Salvius Julianus, there remains a little-known 'dig' on the beach (and abundant plunder in the hotel grounds). But the Romans spoiled things aesthetically by calling it *Putput, Pudput* or *Pupput*. (*Hammamet*, the Arabic name, means variously 'bathing-places' or 'doves'.) Historical mentions are thereafter intermittent.

Strategically prominent between two sheltered bays, the headland was first fortified in 904. Invasion by Roger II's Normans, occupation by the Hafsites, and the Spanish-Corsair confrontation all meant for Hammamet the usual sieges, battles and bloodshed. Seized by Dragut in 1560, blockaded in vain by Andrea Doria, the garrison was in 1602 the victim of a Trojan-horse trick: 300 Knights of Malta landed, disguised as fellow Muslims; they approached, playing Arab pipes and drums, were welcomed with open arms, and promptly sacked the town. When 10 galleons from Sicily and Malta were sighted in 1605, the Muslim inhabitants fled: then turned the historical tables by sending back 100 men, unseen, to decimate the 1,100 invaders.

Hammamet's beach and kasba, stronghold of the medina

By now, in consequence, notorious in Europe – as 'Mahometta or 'La Mahomette' – Hammamet next featured in Tunisia's first 'civil war': leading a revolt against Bey Murad I, a dey known as Hajj Ali Laz retreated here in 1673 – to be killed and buried in the kasba. In 1881, when the French marched in, the townspeople helped repel a first column near by. Though superior forces were soon sent to impose French rule, Hammamet won a tiny final victory, the French commanding officer, Captain Bordier, became so enamoured of the place that he resigned his commission and retired to settle here.

The French built roads and a railway and introduced the telephone. In the Gay Twenties people of means settled into a less brittle life of white villas, antique gardens, warm sands and Siamese cats.

'The Most Beautiful House I Know'

The Romanian Georges Sebastian built what Frank Lloyd Wright called 'the most beautiful house I know'. World War II interrupted things but left little mark: the Foreign Legion garrisoned the kasba, a Senegalese regiment was stationed near by, a couple of bunkers were built up the beach and the Germans – unlike André Gide and Paul Klee, who were invited – installed themselves at Sebastian's. (Von Arnim enjoyed several weeks there but Rommel only three nights.)

Apart from clandestine activity against the French protectorate, and open bloody conflict in 1952, the history of Hammamet since is tourism pure and simple.

The principal landmark remains the **medina**, the old (or Arab) town. Lapped on one side by the sea, its walls back on to the headland cemetery and face the sweep of splendid beach that, colourful with fishing-boats, curves south to the hotels. The ramparts, repeatedly restored, were first erected in 904 by the Aghlabite emir Ibrahim II. But their present parallelogram shape and size – roughly 984 by 360 feet (300 by 100m) – are usually attributed to the Hafsite ruler Abu Zakaria who wanted to protect the Great Mosque he was building in 1236. Enter by the nearest of the three original apertures – the **Bab es-Suq**. Open to infidels since 1881, this 'Market Gate' bends (a medieval means of defence) into the one street of the suq: narrow – donkeys and mobilettes are the only traffic; bright – with carpets, ceramics, embroidery and brassware, and friendly – to say that the shop-boys do not wait for introductions is an understatement.

The first turning left leads into a square that long resisted commercialisation but is now as brash as the rest. Left and off right you see the **Bain Maure** (Turkish bath). Opposite ('Cleanliness being next . . .') stands the **Great Mosque**: 'Entrance Forbidden' to visitors.

Right of the main gate, the first

Citrus fruits strung up for sale in Hammamet

arched entrance in the western wall is not original but dates from the 1960s. It gives on to the Nigro and Boudhina bazaars and thence to the suq. Next, beside the kasba, comes the Bab el Bahar – the original Sea Gate – which nearly every tourist-photographer 'discovers' as a photogenic frame to the fishing-boats and the bay. In the square ahead, where the suq ends, souvenir touts, shops and stalls make of the **Boutique Fella** an even greater haven of sophistication and taste. A lane of jazzy shops runs under the walls to the Marabout of Sidi Bou Hadid. (Its conversion into café is not sacrilege: sipping mint tea and smoking hubble-bubbles on tombs is, as

in Tunis' M'rabet Restaurant, an accepted Tunisian tradition.) Steep steps see you up into the **kasba** (the stronghold or 'keep' of the medieval medina). The courtyard shelters trees, three undated and unmounted cannon, and the Marabout of Sidi Bou Ali (a standard *qubba* – dome with sunken, flag-draped catafalque). Beside the cannon (and the all-important toilets), you climb again to the Chemin de Ronde, the rampart walk. The Moorish café is neat, clean and friendly, the panorama splendid of the old town and the bay. The Martyrs' Memorial is backed by the Nigro Bazaar and upstairs Berbère Restaurant. Through the arch alongside, beneath the cheaper Restaurant de la Poste, the **daily market** offers fruit and

The International Cultural Centre, formerly Sebastian's beautiful house

vegetables, meat, fish and instant chickens killed and plucked to order. A stone's throw up the Avenue de la République you find Boudhina's newspaper shop, the pharmacy and post office on the site of the old Catholic church (1905–72) and, on the near corner, the 'Municipality Musée'.

They mean, of course, the **municipal museum**. Rather better than the spelling, the exhibits are housed in the Marabout of Sidi Ben Issa, which long sheltered not only this worthy's remains but also the local Boy Scouts.

The medina headland divides the two long beaches which the hotels occupy. The roads to them are uninteresting – and definitely too long to walk – so the taxis in their *station privée* just behind the beach will be welcome.

The **Commercial Centre** inland has banks and the Magasin Général (supermarket). Its frontage is *crêperies*, pizzerias and restaurants: Belle-Vue, Fatma, Sand-Pub and the Sonial (not-quite-British) tea room. The Souks d'Art artisanal are the largest of the bazaars behind; a cinema adjoins an *ad hoc* art gallery; cafés serve hubble-bubbles and blaring Arab music; the Playboy claims to be the town's best disco; fountains sometimes play, a blinkered camel turns a patio well-wheel, and there is summer bustle on the restaurant terraces of the upstairs Pergola and Trois Moutons.

An out-of-place period piece alongside, the old Hôtel de la

Plage became the Hôtel de Ville, the town hall. One corner is the Tourist Office. From here the Avenue Habib Bourguiba climbs less interestingly past the police and railway station and on to the southern beach hotels and the **International Cultural Centre**. If no conference is in session and there are no guests in residence, the caretaker may let you enter to see Georges Sebastian's incomparable house: cypress-trees and white colonnades around the cool tiled pool, a refectory table of black monolithic marble, bedrooms of fitted antique mirrors and sunken Roman baths.

Beyond the post office, the Avenue de la République rises through a district called El Haouanet, 'The Shops'. Its only redeeming feature is the **Suq el Khemis**, the weekly market. A pleasantly 'undiscovered' contrast to Nabeul's Friday market, it has steadily outgrown both its allotted place and time: repeatedly shifted round town to larger sites, this Thursday market actually starts on Wednesday afternoon.

A more attractive route to the northern hotels and Nabeul is the **seafront drive** which bends to the beach between the headland cemetery and the Chez Achour Restaurant, a wartime *blockhaus* and the Catholic church.

Accommodation

Hammamet's highest ranking establishments are the **Sindbad**, 4-star luxe (tel: 02 80 122), and **El Manar**, 4-star luxe

(tel: 02 81 333); followed by the **Abou Nawas**, 4-star (tel: 02 81 344), and **Palm Beach**, 4-star (tel: 02 80 333), on the north coast and the **Phenicia**, 4-star (tel: 02 80 331), and the **Shératon**, 4-star (tel: 02 80 555), to the south.

Most holiday-makers prefer 3-star and the choice is correspondingly wider. In the town centre the **Résidence Hammamet**, 3-star (tel: 02 80 408), boasts the only rooftop pool – and looks down on the **Yasmina** opposite, 3-star (tel: 02 80 222). The former is jointly owned and managed with the north-coast **Bel Azur**, 3-star (tel: 02 80 544), and the southern **Les Orangers/Orangers Beach**, 3-star (tel: 02 80 982), all set in ample gardens. Adjoining the last, architecture and gardens make the **Fourati**, 3-star (tel: 02 80 388), the most attractively Tunisian of hotels. Immediately inland, is **Le Hammamet**, 3-star (tel: 02 80 160), which benefits from the attentions of a resident owner, and the **Parc Plage**, 3-star (tel: 02 80 111), and **Continental** (tel: 02 80 456) beside the Cultural Centre, from the resort's most scenically sited pool. Of the new hotels in the southern *zone touristique*, the **Paradis** and **Paradis Résidence**, 3-star (tel: 02 80 300), neighbour the Roman site of Pupput. Just inland, the **Saphir**, 3-star (tel: 02 80 944) – like the **Sultan**, 3-star (tel: 02 80 705) to the north – is aesthetically designed with a single through-view of marble halls, green lawns, and sea. North of the under-rated

Méditerranée, 2-star (tel: 02 80 433), the hotels along the *route touristique El Merazk*a seem to step up: from the low white clusters of **El Fell**, 3-star (tel: 02 80 118), and the **Omar Khayam**, 2-star (tel: 02 80 355), through the **Nozha** *Beach*, 3-star (tel: 02 80 311), and **Dar Khayam**, 3-star (tel: 02 80 454), to the imposing complex of **Les Colombes**, 3-star (tel: 02 80 049), and the **Le Président**, 3-star (tel: 02 81 100).

Festival

The 22 acres (9ha) of park around the International Cultural Centre become public each August for the *Festival International de Hammamet*. Sharing the artistes of the Carthage Festival, the (late) evening performances are held in the mock-Greek theatre which the State, having bought Georges Sebastian's property in 1959, built in 1964.

◆◆◆
NABEUL

In 1738 a Scottish clergyman named Shaw found Nabeul already 'a very thriving town… much celebrated for its potteries'. And it is pottery, far more than the more recent concern for wrought iron, rush-work, perfumes, bricks and tourists, that still preoccupies the modern county-town.

We have not even the name of the original Punic town here, which Agathocles took and which, allied with Carthage, was likewise razed by Scipio after the Third Punic War. Caesar, after triumphing at Thapsus,

established here *Colonia Julia Neapolis*; the emperor Augustus made this colony autonomous – and the builders of Nabeul's first tourist hotel discovered its vestiges by accident in 1964. The hotel's name of Neapolis (since changed to Aquarius) was a foregone conclusion and the resulting excavations (now overgrown again) are visible alongside.

Beyond the bus station, *louage* taxi stand and hospital on the road in from Hammamet, ceramic and pottery shops cluster appropriately round Nabeul's central cross-roads. Straight on, the bustling Avenue Farhat Hached, a sporadic pedestrian precinct, bends between souvenir shops to the main square. Behind the arcades of the suq, rebuilt in 1969, the **Habib Bourguiba**

Mosque is so flawless and typically Tunisian that it may be a surprise to learn that it was in fact American Peace Corps architects who helped with its renovation in 1967. Ahead, Martyrs' Square serves as the loud and crowded entrance to the **Friday Market**. Nabeul is busiest on this Muslim day of rest, its Suq el Juma' being an Arab cross between a street market, a village auction and a jumble sale. Part of this dusty/muddy pandemonium is the 'Kamel Market' for cattle, sheep, goats and camels (too packed and unpredictable for you to photograph properly). You will be outnumbered, jostled but unworried by the hundreds of peasants that ride in each week from miles around.

From the main cross-roads the Avenue Habib Bourguiba runs seaward past pottery shops, the police station, chemist's and the corner Oliviers Restaurant and 'milkbar'. The **mascot-tree** in its giant pot – the tree came first – is a *thuya*, an African member of the conifer family that includes the *arbor vitae*, Tree of Life. Straight on, there is a small **museum** in the public garden. After the turning to the 'Hotel El Ouns', the Khéops and Le Prince, and the Pyramides Hotel, a left-right-left along the beach brings you to the renovated esplanade.

A camel trader in chechia hat, at Nabeul's Friday Market

Accommodation

All 2- or 3-star until the **Khéops**, 4-star luxe, (tel: 02 86 555), opened in 1989 alongside the massive **Les Pyramides**, 3-star (tel: 02 85 775). Next north, behind the esplanade, the **Nabeul Plage**, 3-star (tel: 02 86 111), is also nearest town, then the **Riadh**, 2-star (tel: 02 85 744). Found beyond the holiday-campish **Ramses Résidence,** 2-star (tel: 02 86 644), further flung on the bleak littoral of Dar Chaabane, the **Lido**, 3-star (tel: 02 85 786), is an enterprising hotel and-bungalow complex under Swiss management. Towards Hammamet, the **Prince**, 3-star (tel: 02 85 470), shares a shore of new-built villas, the **Aquarius** caters almost exclusively for French and the **Al Diana Club** for German package parties.

Shopping

Besides all the standard lines, shopping is principally for pottery. With the local clay too coarse or exhausted, the score of 'artist potters' import finer kaolin from Khroumiria and elsewhere. They now use chemical colours from France instead of the old oxidised-metal powders – for designs whose inspiration ranges from ancient Greece through William Morris to Paul Klee. The 'common potters' you find in a fascinating Babylon-clay warren of kilns and shacks in and off the Rue Sidi Barket opposite the Friday market.

CAP BON

This northeastern peninsula that reached out to Sicily was geologically once part of Europe. The sea-channel then between Africa and Europe was the corridor you drive down between Tunis and Hammamet. Cap Bon was the *shora* of ancient Carthage, the 'colonial' hinterland in which the Punic nobles possessed vast farms and vineyards. The Greeks coveted the rich peninsula, their *Ermata Akra*; the Roman empire depended heavily on the produce of this *Mercurii Promontorium*, and still the region relies as much on agriculture as on the tourism concentrated on its southernmost edge, at Nabeul and Hammamet.

While these take advantage of the south coast's broad sandy beaches, the north of Cap Bon is rugged cliffs and coves: a day-tour of the peninsula takes you from the flat and fertile coast of historic Korba, Kelibia and Kerkouane, and past El Haouaria, where the beaches yield to cliffs (and where, from the nearby headland, Sicily is only 87 miles/140 km distant – and on occasions visible). Then, with the 1,404-foot (428m) island-peak of Zembra and its offshoot Zembretta conspicuous off shore, the road rolls on over afforested heathland. Korbous is the only township, clinging to the cliffs of its ravine, before you return to the rich farmlands and citrus groves of Soliman, Grombalia and Hammamet: some grapefruit, better lemons (even sweet, as the *beldi*) but, above all, oranges. From October to May, in a dozen successive varieties, some 200,000 tonnes of Valencia and Maltaise oranges, clementines and mandarins are collected, graded and packed for export in Menzel Bou Zelfa and Soliman, Beni Khalled and Hammamet. Strawberries ripen in June, and apricots and melons, then peaches and figs, grapes and pomegranates... Cap Bon's fresh fruit is an abundant all-year bargain.

KELIBIA

Also known for its fruity *muscat sec*, the Cap Bon town of Kelibia is dominated by its imposing hilltop **fortress**. Reached by the right turn 1½ miles (2.5km) from the town centre, then up the steep stony tracks opposite the port and off the Mansoura road, the edifice (which has bullied the

A hilltop marabout, or holy man's shrine, near Kelibia

coastline for some distance) improves on closer inspection. The tracks converge by the Café el Borj, then rise to the barbican gate.

Punic and Roman remains have been found beneath the present, probably 6th-century Byzantine structure. In 310 BC Agathocles occupied the Punic port which the Greeks had named *Aspis*. Regulus landed here at the start of the First Punic War and, at the end of the Third, the town was destroyed with its ally, Carthage – only to be revived by the Roman empire as *Clupea*. The 9th-century Aghlabites repaired and garrisoned; between 1535 and 1547 the Arab town was three times sacked by the Spaniards, and three times rebuilt. Likewise, partially, by the Turkish pasha Ibrahim Sherif in 1704 and by a local benefactor named Suleiman ben Mustafa in the early 19th century.

Below the castle is the important **fishing-port**, its modernisation being Saudi-backed. Inland, next to the Swedish-financed National School of Fishing, is a Roman excavation area.

Signposted opposite the port, a 2-mile (3km), macadamed cul-de-sac serves the beautiful beach of rocks and silver sand of Mansoura or 'Petit Paris': fine private villas, breezy bungalows and, beneath the clifftop the white elephant of the 'Riviera Kelibia' scheme, El Mansourah Complex.

Accommodation

Best at the above-mentioned **El Mansourah** (tel: 02 96 156), also the **Mamonnia** (tel: 02 96 088), further down the beach. Meanwhile, the **Florida**, 1-star (tel: 02 96 248), has a good deal of character and good fish cuisine.

Festival

Kelibia's international Amateur Film festival currently shows over 100 entries from some 40 countries (biennial, in July).

◆◆
KERKOUANE

The lowly ruins here that stretch along the Cap Bon cliffs constitute the best-preserved Punic town in Africa. A broad semicircular talus, or slope (from the ramparts) encloses the compact settlement. Its main street runs parallel to the cliffs and low restored walls mark off not only houses but individual rooms. Water-channels and sunken baths are still clear in the flooring; floors, and even the built-in baths and benches, are often farmhouse-kitchen red in colour, with white tesserae and sometimes cobalt-blue glass. Oven relics inside the first talus – red sherds and charred pits – actually indicate kitchens. Also inside the talus, a curious Tanit mosaic inlaid in the flooring is the traditional depiction of this goddess (the Phoenicians' Astarte).

Preparing to greet the migrants: El Haouaria's Falconry Festival parades each June

All the above is typical Punic domestic: since the 5th-century BC site was 'discovered' in 1952, the only public edifice exposed is what might have been a temple. The absence of administrative buildings led to the guide-book idea that Kerkouane was a Punic seaside resort: longer heads suggested that any such holiday camp would hardly have needed the nearby necropolis, excavated in 1968–9 and again in the 1980s. An exemplary museum now documents and complements the mostly unspectacular but well-maintained site.

◆
EL HAOUARIA

Facing the sunset, El Haouaria leans sleepily against the cliffs of Jebel Abiod, the headland of Cap Bon. But it rouses itself each June for the **Sparrow-Hawk Festival** (see below). At other times, if you happen to be passing, it is worth a visit mostly for its **Roman quarries** (along the main Avenue Habib Bourguiba, across the central Place de la République, up between the cemetery and the marabouts of Sidi Ben Issa and Sidi Bou Ayesh, and right as the hilltop track forks, roughly a mile/1.5km from the village). The spot, once desolately beautiful, where tall orange cliffs meet the sea, has been spoilt with breeze-block walls and a pink drink-stall. There are four interconnected caves: the largest with a crudely hacked camel, the second with a hole full of daytime bats, and all with ceiling shafts and footholds for removing the rock.

Festival

The Cap Bon peninsula ends in Jebel Abiod (the White Mountain), and this in the headland of Ras Addar. Here, where the hawk-eyed can (they say) see Sicily, migrating birds gather in thousands each spring for the return flight to Europe by the shortest sea-crossing. To celebrate the event, El-Haouaria holds the Sparrow-Hawk Festival: parades of floats and fanfares pass the visiting dignitaries in the village square and, on the hill, an odd competition is held in which hawks are launched after captive larks and quail.

Restaurants

The best/only place to lunch (or use the toilet) is the **Restaurant de l'Épervier** (sparrow-hawk), in the main street facing the *Association Nationale des Fauconniers* (the Falconers).

◆◆
KORBOUS

Korbous and its coastline pose the dilemma of whether to publicise how lovely they are and perhaps end their surprising peacefulness (the place being only 30 miles/48km from Tunis), or keep them quietly to yourself. The small spa takes its thermal mission seriously. Families came from Roman Carthage to take the waters here at *Aquae Calidae Carpitanae* just as Tunisians and foreigners do today. Its popularity then lapsed for centuries until Ahmed Bey built the pavilion that in 1901 became the present *Établissement Thermal* and the

French civil engineer Lecore Carpentier began the development of the modern town. His villa still stands on the highest peak as you approach. Old Korbous, with its colonnaded and arched hostelries, is now confined to the left slope of the single street. The right-hand side is wholly 'medico-modern': the rebuilt Clinique Médicale des Thermes and the sand-coloured, green and white blocks of the Hôtel des Sources. Downhill, below the souvenir shacks and in the rebuilt block of **Ain Araga**, stairs and a tunnel lead to the ex-Roman *étuves* ('sweating-rooms').

At the Ain Atrous spring sulphurous water shoots out of a mountain beyond the little spa of Korbous

Here, in Stygian heat and steam, you can lie for as long as you need to cure obesity and/or sterility (men in the morning, women in the afternoon). The seafront focal centre is the **Ain Chefah bath-house**, originally beylical but extended in the 1970s. Left of the car park lies the sunken, tiled and balustraded **Ain Sebia** (Virgin's Spring), where bowls of water are available free. Along the road, 1 mile (1.5km) on from the bath-house, **Ain Atrous** (Goat's Spring) is curious: rushing out of a Greek oracle site in the cliff face, 120°F (50°C) water streams down the rocks leaving mineral streaks and a strong whiff of sulphur.

Accommodation
Adequate enough in the hillside **Hôtel des Sources**, 3-star

(tel: 02 94 533). The better designed rooms and panoramic seascapes of the older **Ain Oktor**, 3-star (tel: 02 94 557), contrast oddly with a clientele in large part convalescent.

◆◆
ZAGHOUAN

County-town since 1978 of the governorate of the same name, Zaghouan is fast expanding into a sizeable mountainside metropolis with administrative and ministry buildings.
As you climb in steeply from Hammamet, veer sharp left above the sorry-looking **arch** (2nd-century AD), a relic of Roman *Ziqua*. It is remarkable solely for its two alcoves (from which Roman statues once looked out over the valley) and its simplistic cow's head on the keystone. The main Rue Habib Bourguiba climbs to the Place Habib Bourguiba; behind the **Jami' el Kebir el Jedid** (the New Great Mosque, 1982), the ex-church has a fine view. By the quaint fountain, the narrow Rue Sidi Ali Azouz climbs past the old **Great Mosque** to the arched and exquisite, early 19th-century **Qubba of Sidi Ali Azuz**. Above the Hanifi mosque's cupola and the Marabout of Sidi Saad, the road levels out at the Martyrs' Memorial, with the lawcourt and Ministry of Agriculture and the Marabout of Sidi Hashlaf at the top of the hill. The rustic lane climbs to a T-junction: left for the Hôtel des Nymphes and right to the Nymphaeum. The Roman **Temple of the Waters**, built under Hadrian, retains its walls with their 12 niches for statues but is defaced by modern graffiti and 'restorations' (the latest, not so ugly, being the neatly blocked, hourglass-shaped basin).

Accommodation
The scenic, pine-fragrant **Hôtel des Nymphes**, 2-star (tel: 02 75 094), where business is such that the bungalows below the main block are not only always available but also for sale.

◆◆◆
THUBURBO MAIUS ✓

Thuburbo is one of the few sites where the guide is recommended – not for any great expertise on his part but because of the topography. Untroubled by earthquakes and rich from the corn land around, Thuburbo grew steadily from a settled Berber site to a Phoenician city that sided with Carthage in the final Punic War. Punitively taxed but not demolished by Scipio, the town was chosen in 27 BC for one of Octavius' colonies of veterans. The prosperous *Julia Aurelia Commoda* of the 2nd century AD declined in the 3rd; revived in the 4th century by Constantine II, the *Respublica Felix* fell victim to the Vandals and was abandoned in Byzantine times. 'Rediscovered' in 1875, the fine ruins were unearthed and re-erected only in 1912.
Most conspicuous from the entrance are the 28-foot (8m) columns of the **capitol** (AD 168); monumental stairs lead up from the 160-foot (49m) square **forum** (AD 161–92, restored in 376).

*The fine ruins of Thuburbo Maius,
unearthed and re-erected in 1912*

Deep chambers behind the capitol contain oil-presses: as Rome declined, tradesmen and peasants moved in and made workshops of the imperial monuments. Off the south corner of the forum is the paved *agora* (market-place) and to the southwest the **Temple of Mercury** (AD 211) with its circle of eight column stumps. Southeast from the market lie the imposing **Winter Baths** (20 rooms, four-column portico, mosaic-floored *frigidarium*, pools circular and square and latrines with a rectangle of urinals). Due west then the **Petronii Portico**, built in AD 225 by Petronius Felix and Sons. Here was found the Bardo Museum's 'podgy boxers' mosaic, which identified this show-piece as a *palaestra* (gymnasium). (You can see a Latin Lexicon-game, '36 Letters', on the paving in the southernmost corner.) Southwest again, the larger **Summer Baths** (30,000 square feet/2,800sq m of more extensive marble and mosaic, three baths, and all restored in AD 361).

♦♦♦
DOUGGA ✓

Dougga dominates Tunisian archaeology – for its site, entirety and extent. Bulla Regia half hides underground, Thuburbo Maius lies low in its valley, but at 2,000 feet (600m) Dougga's 62 acres (25ha) of monuments are equal to the pre-eminence. Its theatres, temples, thermae and capitol all overlook the deep Oued Khalled and exploit the panorama.

Whether you come up the well-paved road from Teboursouk or the stony track from Nouvelle Dougga, the **Temple of Saturn** stands unforgettable on the skyline. Behind the landmark of its three and a half columns, the temple (AD 195) has subterranean vaults, a central area pell-mell with masonry, and an odd imprint of man-size feet in the paving. The road below ends – where visitors park and the would-be guides wait – by the **theatre**. Built in AD 166–9, it had a reputed capacity of 3,500, which is about the minimum house now at the **Dougga Festival** each June. Opposite the custodian's quarters – where a tip secures a sight of actual Roman food – steps descend into a Roman shopping street. Look down: the paving is pierced by central drains, scored on the inclines to hold the horses' hooves and rutted with the passage of countless chariot wheels. The street opens out into the **Square of the Winds**, laid between AD 180 and 192 and named from the 25-foot (8m) wide 'compass' of winds inscribed in the paving in the 3rd century. Southwards, below the mosque, a paved alley crosses the market and a lower area of mosaics, columns and house-walls, and 22 steps descend into the colonnaded 'changing-rooms' and the lofty halls of the 3rd-century **Licinian Baths**.

Adjoining the Square of the Winds, the *area ante Capitolium* precedes the incomparable **Capitol**, built in AD 167 in honour of Jupiter, Juno and Minerva and now one of the finest remains of Roman North Africa. Beyond its monumental 32-foot (10m) wide stairs, humbler steps take you into the **forum**, enclosed by the Byzantines with Roman stone. From the west end of the forum an easily recognisable 'rampart walk' runs back below the capitol and past the rectangular doorway of the **House of Asheb** (AD 164–6, possibly the slave market – and vantage point for the standard postcard view of the capitol), the **Temple of Tellus** (AD 261) and a dark tunnel leading into the baths, to rejoin the main track below the second theatre.

Dougga's vast Capitol, dedicated to Jupiter, Juno and Minerva

Cross the main track, descend the steps and continue down the paved lane to the second **baths**. The focal centre of these 'Thermae of the Cyclops' is inevitably the horseshoe of 12 toilet seats in the communal latrine. The 15 inches (38cm) between the apertures seem to indicate that the occupants were either diminutive or pressed knee to knee. Beside the baths (or down the 21 steps from the small track below the main baths) stands the 3rd-century **House of the Trifolium**. Couriers talk enthusiastically about this, 'the best-preserved of Dougga's family mansions': it was most probably the brothel. The proof has been removed to spare blushes: Roman fishmongers sculpted a fish on their counter as trade-mark; in brothels, the obvious phallus.
Open: Tuesday to Sunday 09.30–16.30hrs.

Accommodation
Only in **Thugga Hotel**, 2-star (tel: 08 65 713), 4 miles (6km) away in Teboursouk.

LE KEF
Le Kef ('The Rock') is unofficially 'capital' of the western border region. In this dependency of Carthage, first recorded in 256 BC, the army of mercenaries assembled and mutinied after the First Punic War. The Roman colony of *Sicca Veneria* which the emperor Octavian established here took its name from a temple to Venus/Astarte in which the 'Punic matrons'

practised sacred prostitution. Paradoxically, the 2nd–3rd-century *colonia* became an important Christian centre, and monasteries, as in Europe, meant material prosperity. The Arab invasion put an end to both; only with the Turkish regency was Le Kef re-animated as a beylical bulwark against the pashas of Algiers.
The main street follows a contour of the cliff, so steep that most side-roads are stepped. From its northern end you fork uphill beside the presidential palace. The **Zawia of Sidi Abdul-Qader** (1834) has a fine minaret and five cupolas but is no longer the library its plaque proclaims. Here either fork left along the Rue Ali ben Trad to the Mosque of Sidi Bou Makhlouf, the old Great Mosque and the renovated **basilica** which, besieged by statuary, capitals and plinths, has become a lapidary museum. Or go right, past the dinky minaret – the palace's power transformer! – to the **Regional Museum of Popular Arts and Traditions** which contains an evocative replica of a nomad encampment. Follow the 'contour' beyond the museum for the 14th-century **Mosque of Sidi Bou Makhlouf**, its interior a sculpted-plaster masterpiece. Built by Mohammed Bey in 1679, with ramparts added by Ali Bey in the 1740s, the **kasba** crowns Le Kef. With imposing portal, magnificent bastions and inscribed columns, it has been restored to function as a tourist centre, complete with rooms and refreshments.

SOUSSE AND THE SAHEL

◆◆◆
SOUSSE

Sousse is, as far as tourists are
concerned, a compromise
between Tunis and Hammamet,
a city in its own right like the
former, a popular resort like the
latter. If the beaches, although
excellent, are not as exquisite
as Hammamet's, and the Sahel
hinterland of sebkha and
olive-groves less exotic,
Sousse's medina, museum and
catacombs, its esplanade,
cinemas and pavement cafés,
its prestigious adjunct of
Kantaoui (otherwise known as
Sousse-Nord), all give it the

*The Great Mosque of Kairouan,
Tunisia's holiest and oldest Arab
city, and the fourth most revered in
Islam*

variety that Hammamet lacks.
The city's past is
correspondingly varied. Before
Carthage but after Utica, the
Phoenicians established here a
port of unknown name, and
near this flourishing town – a
large *tophet* has been found –
Hannibal disembarked at the
end of his elephantine
campaign in Italy. For
repudiating Carthage in the
Third Punic War, Sousse was
made a 'free city' by Scipio – an
honour which it thereafter lost

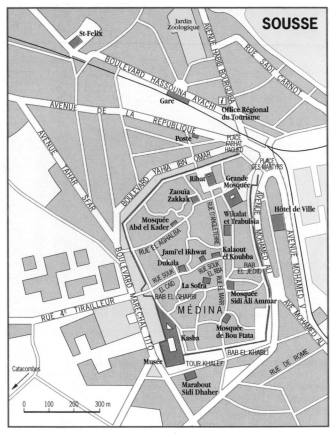

SOUSSE

for supporting Pompey's allies against Caesar. The Vandals renamed the now-Christian town *Hunericopolis*, the Byzantines *Justinianopolis*. The Arabs reduced it to *Susa* and temporary oblivion. Having embarked here for their conquest of Sicily, the Aghlabites then built extensively (*ribat*, kasba and Great Mosque), even though Sousse remained Kairouan's rival and, during the beylical civil war of the 1730s, Tunis' rival, too. The town was attacked by Ali Pasha's gunboats, as it had been by the 12th-century Normans and the 16th-century Spaniards – and was to be yet again by the Genoese, the French and finally the Allies. Their heavy attacks in 1943 led to the necessary rebuilding of the modern town.

The **Place Farhat Hached** is very visibly the city's hub. To seaward, ships loom disconcertingly close. Opposite, a marabout shelters the Information Bureau on the corner of the Boulevard M'hamed Maarouf, which splits round the post office. On the next tangent, where the taxis and hippomobiles wait, the Boulevard Hassouna Ayachi rises between the Farès Hotel and the **railway station** to the **Church of St Felix** (a sweet, white chapel with its Stations of the Cross slit-eyed in plaster and a more artistic marble Last Supper). And opposite, beside the taxi rank, is the main Avenue Habib Bourguiba. As if all this did not ensure constant commotion, the railway line to Sfax runs plumb across the square.

The **Avenue Habib Bourguiba** begins with the Regional Tourist Office, the Monoprix store and the Café Olympique, where the youths sit watching the pretty girls for whom the town is known. (Beyond the café, towards the port, arcades stretch past the Malouf and Bonheur restaurants to the Hadrumète Hotel.) There follows the bookshop, the chemist and the Musée du Tapis store. After the misnamed Claridge Hotel, cinemas and Tunis Air, the police station occupies a side-street, and the Sousse Palace Hotel the site of the old French prison. Opposite, Les Sportifs is good for a cheap lunch or dinner, while the Gourmet and Calèche restaurants hide up side-streets. Then travel agencies and car-hire firms, banks, more bazaars and the 'Atlantik Pub'.

Ahead, the seafront *corniche* is lively in summer but otherwise desultory. The perennial bustle keeps to the parallel Avenue Taïeb Mehiri. Opposite the 'Police Secours' ('Help!') in the Zawia of Sidi Jaaffar are the Justinia and Justinia Nour hotels. Meeker rivals are the Saïd, Africa Beach, Corniche and Ennacim; the 'Aparthotel' Okba occupies most of Sousse's Colisée complex. Even more complex, after the Karawan Hotel, is the Néjma, a vast split-level edifice of 'hotel résidence' and shops, restaurant, snack bar and Yamama disco, the *Magasins Modernes*' efficient

Built in the 8th century, the ribat of Monastir combined religious and military functions (see page 58)

supermarket and a suq of boutiques pointing to the beach. Empty plots along the way are slowly filling with bazaars, and lowly grocers and *gargotes* are yielding to restaurants: the Flouca and a 'Fast Food' with mock-McDonald arches; the Ambassadeur, Pacha, and the good Chinese Hong-Kong and Le Phénicien, then the Tiptop, Albatros, Escargot and Baraka restaurants.

Sousse Medina Across the Place Farhat Hached from the main avenue, you enter the old town by the Place des Martyrs, the breach of the one-time Bab el Bahar made in the walls by the bombing of 1943. Here stands Selmi's pink-plaster retort to Rodin's *Burghers of Calais*: eight figures representing the 12 Sousse martyrs of January 1952.

The Great Mosque
Unmistakable with its kiosk-minarets. A courtyard of galleries, the southernmost added in 1675 and all renovated in 1975, then the prayer-room, one of the most impressive you will see: impressive in its simplicity, not in its decoration. Built in 851, the prayer-room was extended in the 10th, 11th and 17th centuries and restored in 1964–5. ('Open to the No-Moslem people every Day from 8 am to 1 pm. . . . Decently dressed people only are allowed to visit'.)

Prominent opposite is the **ribat**, most important of the monastery-fortresses with which the Aghlabites picketed the coast from Ceuta to Alexandria to forestall Christian attacks. Sousse's *ribat* was completed in 821 (at a cost of 18,000 dinars). You enter by the barbican gate, with four apertures above for the portcullis and/or boiling oil: a plain and reworked courtyard, a first gallery of cells – their antique contents now removed to Kairouan – and, beneath the Kufic inscription above its entrance, 73 steps up the *Nador* (watch-tower). Used for spotting enemy aircraft in World War II, it offers the best view of the new town and the old.

Behind the Great Mosque and the Médina Hotel (quaint but noisy) the Rue Averroès becomes the **Rue de Paris**, Sousse's suq of souvenirs. Number 54 is the Wikalat et-Trabulsia, a two-storey courtyard – like a Baghdad *khan* – built in the 1640s. Straight on, in the Rue el Marr, the **Mosque of Sidi Ali Ammar** is marginally interesting with its façade probably dating from the 10th century.

Better turn right, between the Suq er-Rebaa Mosque and its *midha* (toilet). This **Rue Souk el Rbâ** is surprisingly narrow for the medina's main thoroughfare. The 'vegetable market' is a misnomer – this Souk el Khadra sells shoes. It leads to the jewellery suq, well stocked and glittering with gold. Go second right uphill to find the very restored **Qalaat el Qubba (Kalaout el Koubba)**, its 10th-century cupola curiously gadrooned. The suq becomes the Rue Souk el Caid ('Tunisian Parfum', right under the arches) and climbs, so steeply that it needs steps, between booths of metalware and bric-à-brac, past the incongruous complex of the **Jami' el Ikhwat** (the Mosque of the Sisters) and the Oukala nightclub, to the ramparts at the **Bab el Gharbi**, the Western Gate. Turn left along the outside of the bastions and battlements to the **kasba**.

The **museum** (*open*: Tuesday to Sunday 09.00–12.00hrs, 15.00–18.30hrs; 14.00–17.30hrs in winter) here is a smaller, more digestible Bardo (see page 27). The main patio has a garden and attractive mosaics: of horses complete with reins and bridles and of Neptune with fish, squids and octopus (also from Sousse). Between them and in the next gallery is less-sophisticated 3rd–5th-century work, much with Christian anchors, doves, grapes, fish, labarum-signs, inverted swastikas and '*In Pace*'. The impressive long room off this gallery has almost 50 mosaics. In the furthest gallery the 5th–6th-century tiles, all between 10 and 11 inches (25 and 28cm) square, once decorated Christian basilicas with Adam and Eve, beasts, and saints on horseback. And off this gallery, a room of Punic stelae from the *tophet* (crematorium) of Sousse, where by the 2nd century BC animals were replacing the sacrificial infants . . . *Molchomor* instead of *Moloch* (see page 10).

Beyond, a gallery leads (right) into rooms of mosaics, amphorae and terracotta tomb equipment – two 3rd-century BC Punic tombs even *in situ* below – and (ahead) to the gardens, toilets and rooms installed with painted frescoes and more fine mosaics.

Worth finding – a mile or so (1.5km) west of Sousse – are the **catacombs**, burial place of early Christians from the 2nd–5th centuries. The 240 galleries of 15,000 tombs extend for over 3 miles (5km). The catacombs may be visited whenever the *gardien* can be found.

Accommodation

Sousse's seafront of owner-operated establishments, built by local businessmen, has mushroomed most noticeably around the Hana and Marhaba complexes. The former (which now also runs Sousse-Nord's Hannibal Palace) dominates the out-of-town end of Sousse's

Parades fill Sousse's seafront for the Festival of Aoussou (Neptune)

esplanade with the curling concrete cluster of the **Chems El Hana**, 4-star (tel: 03 28 190), the **El Hana**, 4-star (tel: 03 25 818), and **El Hana Beach**, 3-star (tel: 03 26 900). The Marhaba complex is nearest to town of the north-coast establishments, the **Marhaba Beach**, 4-star (tel: 03 40 112), being the latest, smartest adjunct to the **Marhaba**, 3-star (tel: 03 42 170), **Marhaba Club**, 3-star (tel: 03 42 170), **Tour Khalef**, 3-star (tel: 03 41 844), and, further north, the **Salem**, 2-star (tel: 03 41 966). Beside and between these stand the non-chain, family-run hotels: the **Hill Diar**, 3-star (tel: 03 21 286), **Scheherazade**, 3-star (tel: 03 41 433), **Samara** (tel: 03 23 699), and **Alyssa**, 2-star (tel: 03 40 715). Town-centre hotels near the public beach are the vastly improved **Justinia** and **Justinia Nour**, 3-star (tel: 03 26 888), towards the port, the shabby but well-sited **Hadrumète**, 2-star (tel: 03 26 291), and the **Ennacim**, 2-star (tel: 03 27 100), **Farés** (tel: 03 27 380), and **Okba** (tel: 03 25 522).

Festival

For the annual Festival of Aoussou (Neptune) everyone goes, quite literally, to town. Every July/August, floats from the hotels, businesses and European twin towns; Zlass horsemen and local musicians; 20-foot (6m) giants in papier mâché; bikini-clad tourists on camels; toy trains, old cars and you, if you want to – all parade along the esplanade to the Place Farhat Hached.

SOUSSE-NORD

El Kantaoui, *alias* 'Sousse North', has added a new dimension to Tunisian tourism. With the country established as a popular 'package' destination, the authorities opted in the mid-1970s for a bold new approach: to create, on a scenic but 'virgin' stretch of coast, a self-contained holiday complex in which a marina and a tournament **golf course** would constitute 'up-market' attractions. With help from Abu Dhabi, Kuwait and the World Bank, their El Kantaoui project is succeeding. Around the 10-acre (4ha), 340-berth **marina**, the 'first Mediterranean garden port', with arched, cobbled alleys, gardened squares and lamplit quays, has already an 'old world' charm. Waterfront boutiques and duty-free shops, banks, cafés and good restaurants like des Emirs cater for yachtsmen and the cosmopolitan owners of the 'Houses by the Sea'. As well as a clinic and chemist's, officialdom is discreetly there with Customs, police and post office. Lanes wind to the Escale Restaurant, La Tour disco and *Magasin Général* supermarket.

Accommodation

If Hammamet's hotels are restful, *reposant*, Sousse-Nord's are *imposant*, overwhelmingly, even dauntingly imposing. The first (run initially by Trust House Forte) was the Arabo-magnificent **Hannibal Palace**, 4-star luxe (tel: 03 41 577), which looks down on the adjacent **Hasdrubal**, 4-star (tel: 03 41 944), and the **Bulla Regia**, 3-star (tel: 03 40 922), the humble hotel-training hotel. As competition for the Hannibal Palace (and an ego-trip for the architect or owner), there is the **Marhaba International**, 4-star (tel: 03 43 633), with breath-taking marble columns. Inland, **El Kanta**, 4-star (tel: 03 40 466), has friendly efficiency, the **Green Park**, 4-star (tel: 03 43 277), a stylish 1930s décor, near-miss art deco. The **Diar El Andalous**, 4-star luxe (tel: 03 46 200), and its self-catering **Club Alhambra** (tel: 03 40 900) are part of the Kuwaiti-financed Abou Nawas chain, while north along the road to Hergla the **Abou Sofiane**, 3-star (tel: 03 46 444), the **Mouradi**, 3-star (tel: 03 46 355), and the **Selima Club** (tel: 03 40 080) surround and outclass the older **Club El Kantaoui** (tel: 03 42 011).

Monastir's Cotusal salt-works

◆◆◆
MONASTIR ✓

For 30 years revered (and splendiferously restored) as birthplace of ex-president Bourguiba, Monastir means for most visitors today the first aerial glimpse of Tunisia. For with very few exceptions all charter flights from Europe (and several scheduled services) now use the Habib Bourguiba International Airport of Monastir-Skanes.

Part of that view looming through the aircraft window is the salt-works' strangely red 'pans' of sea-water. Beside the road to Sousse, the hills of evaporated, dried and processed salt are also odd white sights.

You may well come in low over Monastir itself: its battlements, minarets, towers and cupolas make of it a theatrical back-cloth larger than life. The settlement's start in life as Punic *Rous Penna*; Caesar's garrison of *Ruspina*; the town's 11th-century (but temporary) replacement of Kairouan as Tunisia's religious capital; its key defensive position throughout the Middle Ages; the Muslim soldiers' belief that three days' garrison duty in this first ribat-town vouchsafed them Paradise . . . all were of less importance in Tunisian eyes than the fact that Habib Bourguiba was born here in 1903 (or perhaps 1901) – on 3 August, anyway.

The **Bourguiba family mausoleum** is still the township's unmistakable focal centre. The resplendent shrine of buff stone, blue ceramics and Carrara marble was rebuilt even bigger in 1978. In 1980 came the twin minarets, grey marble and gold-tipped; then the four gadrooned domes, one dazzling golden, three gilded green behind (in honour of the ex-president's father, mother and first wife). The road rises inland past two open-polygonal 'kiosks', one the **Martyrs' Memorial**. Amidst the tombs behind, the Qubba of Sidi Ali el Mezeri (a 12th-century imam) has the reputation of curing ailing babies and of being imbued afresh each Friday morning with a divine aroma. In the background looms the

The Martyrs' Memorial at Monastir

Ribat (one of the monastery-fortresses in which the early *murabitin* – those 'bound' to Islam – lived, prayed and prepared themselves for martyrdom fighting the Christian 'infidels'). In more recent times, ironically, this *ribat* has served more often as an Old Testament film-set: opening in 1976 with Zeffirelli's *Life of Christ* and doubling for Monty Python's *Life of Brian*, starring with Ava Gardner in *Anno Domini* and appearing in Roman Polanski's *Pirates*. Built in 796 by Harthema ibn Ayun, a general with Harun ar-Rashid, the *ribat* has been rebuilt or reworked four times (in the 9th, 11th, 17th and 19th centuries) and now requires expert study to say precisely what came when. Suffice it to say that from the northern ramparts of the Men's Ribat, by which you enter, there is a fine view of the cemetery, and from the *Nador* (watch-tower), with its 87 steps, an even better panorama of the town. The former mosque between the Men's Ribat and the Women's (to the south) is an Islamic Museum.
Open: summer: 08.00–19.00hrs; winter: 09.00–12.00hrs, 14.00–18.00hrs
Closed: Mondays.
The elegant ONA store, opposite in the demolished Bab Derb, is eclipsed by the model **Mosque of Habib Bourguiba** (1963–6). Only the courtyard is open. The window-grilles have been blocked: of the marble fountains and paving in the courtyard, the 19 teak doors sculpted in Kairouan, the 86 gleaming columns and

magnificent chandeliers in the prayer-room… not even a peep is possible.

Left is an area which Spanish designers, having finished with the mosque, developed into a 'Moorish' tourist quarter (which houses Tunis Air and the 'Tourisme Information'). Ahead on the Place de l'Indépendance, fork half-right for the **Bab el Gharbi** (the Western Gate) and the road back to Skanes.

Accommodation

Centred on nearby Skanes (see below). In Monastir itself there is the plush modern **Regency**, 4-star luxe (tel: 03 60 033), and **El Habib**, 4-star (tel: 03 62 944), the more economical **Esplanade**, 3-star (tel: 03 61 147), and the idiosyncratic **Yasmin**, 1-star (tel: 03 62 511).

◆◆
SKANES (SKANÈS)

Monastir's beach hotels are scattered amongst the palm-gardens of Skanes which – apart from the hilltop Sayada Mosque, the airport and the ex-president's favourite palace – consists almost exclusively of beach hotels in palm-gardens.

Accommodation

Opposite the airport (where night flights are infrequent), the **Kuriat Palace**, 4-star (tel: 03 61 200), has a breathtaking entrance, all fountains and pink marble. The neighbouring **Skanes Palace**, 4-star (tel: 03 61 350) is older and more functional, the **Dkhila Jockey Club**, 4-star (tel: 03 61 833), an 'animated' Meridien hotel,

and the **Skanes El Hana**, 4-star (tel: 03 62 055), all stylish concrete. The **Sahara Beach**, 3-star (tel: 03 61 088), leads the 3-star establishments, with three seven-storey blocks each bigger than many hotels and a mainly British clientele. On the same Dkhila beach, its neighbours are the **Tropicana Club**, 3-star (tel: 03 60 554), the **Ruspina**, 3-star (tel: 03 61 360), and **Tanit**, 2-star (tel: 03 64 791). The **Club Méditerranée** is reserved for *gentils membres* booked from Europe, the **Chems** and **Rivage** for French union members, pensioners etc. The **Robinson Club**, 4-star (tel: 03 31 055), **Abou Nawas Sun Rise**, 3-star (tel: 03 27 144), **El Houda**, 2-star (tel: 03 25 340) and **Sangho Farah**, 2-star (tel: 03 66 190), form a new *zone touristique* along the beach north towards Sousse.

◆◆
MAHDIA

The modern county-town-cum-fishing-port and canning centre occupies a promontory historically important. Both Phoenicians and Romans appreciated it as a naval base; the Fatimites exploited it as an easily defended capital. The Arab historian Ibn Khaldun praised it as a 'dagger held in the fist', while his French contemporary Froissart went one better by calling the headland 'Africa' *tout court*. (The name survives in this *Cap Africa*.) The site saved the Mahdi in 944–5 from an eight-month siege by the Kharijite horde of Abu Yazid

Mahdia's headland cemetery

(whom he crucified on the Skifa el Kahla then stuffed with straw). The Zirites fled here in 1057 as the Beni Hilal neared Kairouan. Roger II's Norman forces evicted them in 1148, only to be ousted in their turn by the Almohads 12 years later. In 1390 a Franco-Genoese fleet failed to take the port, which was occupied by Dragut in 1549 and, after triple bombardment, by Charles V from 1550 to 1554. The deys and beys brought new blood, several local families descending from the Turks' janissaries and other Balkan subjects. Under the French protectorate Mahdia grew into Tunisia's foremost fishing-port and, with the Sahel's olive-oil and the salt worked locally until 1938, its largest canning centre.

The **Avenue Habib Bourguiba**, the town's main street, shies right of the massive Skifa el Kahla and, between the town hall and the Mosque of Sidi Mteir, opens to the **fishing-port**. The long, modern, orderly quay becomes a lively market every Friday morning,

for clothes, fruit, vegetables and local essentials such as camel saddles.

Equally colourful on Friday mornings too, the *Bab Zouila* belies its alias of **Skifa el Kahla** (Sombre Gate). Rebuilt in 1554, it is the only remnant of the 35-foot (10m) thick wall by which the hated Mahdi shut off his isthmus capital. The Friday morning **market** here is unique: village women hawking their gilt and sequinned *gilets de mariage*, while pedlars squat weighing out gold and silver.

The **medina** beyond is crossed by the Rue Abdallah el Mehdi, which is flanked by jewellers, clothes and shoe shops, a pinball saloon and a booth offering '*Coiffure et Circoncision*'. Next the Mosque of Hajji Mustafa Hamza and that, with a newer and taller minaret, of his brother Suleiman Hamza further left.

Opposite, with no minaret at all, the **Great Mosque** is simply a masterpiece of its kind: well-proportioned, dignified and unadorned. It was founded by Ubaid-Allah in 921. In the courtyard the Zirites massacred his Shi'ite co-religionists in 1016, thereby incurring the Fatimite caliph's wrath – and prompting the Hilalian invasion. The same courtyard was made a Spanish cemetery by Charles V, who used the mosque as a stop-gap church, and blew it up when he departed in 1554. Sporadically patched up thereafter, the edifice had collapsed utterly by the 1950s, whence the complete 1960s reconstruction in perfect imitation Fatimite.

The cliff road beyond – a *circuit touristique* – climbs past the excavations of Ubaid-Allah's palace and the domeless Marabout of Sidi Senubri to the **Borj el Kebir** (the Headland Tower). Worked in the façade is a cross-bow and a caricature tiger. The strategically winding entrance of this one-time French prison contains antiquarian photographs and capitals; a museum is planned for the hall, and the crenellated walls are panoramic.

Accommodation
Classiest is the Abou Nawas chain's **Club Cap Mahdia**, 3-star (tel: 03 80 300), homeliest is the **Mehdi**, 3-star (tel: 03 81 683), a bold 3-storey block that monopolises the esplanade.

Festival
The courtyard of the Borj el Kebir is the setting of the annual *Nuits de Mahdia* ('Mahdia Nights') – July 'folklore' and *Son et Lumière*.

◆◆◆

EL JEM ✔

The world's sixth largest **Roman amphitheatre** here – arguably finer than the Colosseum in Rome – is easy to visualise whole.

> **Fight or Die**
> The three tiers of arcades could seat some 30,000 spectators. The games became famous and drew crowds from much of Roman Africa. They would file in by the vaulted galleries and the steep stairs around; the emperor would take his place and, from the dungeons below, the gladiators and Christian martyrs, incarcerated for days beside the lions, would be brought out to fight or die.

El Jem acquired the inevitable legends: a tunnel to Mahdia – still to be unearthed – was large enough for elephants to drag up the imported rock for building, but too narrow for them to turn back; another led to the catacombs of Sousse. The Romans built this colossus in AD 230 – 484 feet (148m) long, 403 feet (123m) wide, 117 feet (36m) high – to persuade the resurgent Berbers that Rome was not declining. Gordian was 80 and senile when the local landlords, proclaimed him emperor here in AD 238. He reigned for a few weeks before being defeated by the emperor Maximinus, losing his son and killing himself at Carthage. The amphitheatre was probably not the scene of the legendary last stand of El Kahena, the Berbers' 7th-century woman leader, as many believe, and the walls were first breached by the ruler Mohammed Bey, to evict rebels hiding here in 1695. Closed from 1974 to 1980 for restorations partly financed by the Gulbenkian Foundation, the site is now open daily from dawn to dusk.

◆◆
SFAX
This, Tunisia's second largest city, is part industrial, part historic. It was heavily bombed in World War II – its fine Hôtel de Ville (town hall) remaining as the blocks around went down – and widely rebuilt. Their compatriots look on the Sfaxis as slightly untypical: thrifty, hard-working, shrewd (*Baccalauréat* passes here are the country's best) and somehow more Nordic than Mediterranean.

This may explain their constant prosperity since Roman times. Most vestiges of the Roman *Taparura* are in the Hôtel de Ville Museum. Better preserved, and Sfax's main claim to 'beauty', are the 9th-century walls of the Aghlabite medina. Thanks perhaps to its long-established wealth from olives, cereals, cloth, fruit, fish and perfume, the 'Capital of the South' alone survived as an independent state after the Hilalian invasion. True to that tradition, it backed Ali ben Ghedahem's revolt against the bey in 1864 and succumbed to the French in 1881 only after naval bombardment. Its commercial significance increased when Sfax became the railhead for the line to Metlaoui's phosphate mines. Deposits of oil discovered both on shore and off have, since the mid-1970s, given the city's fortunes a further fillip.

The **Hôtel de Ville Museum** on the corner of Avenues Bourguiba and Hedi Chaker merits a visit. Besides the usual coins, terracotta, frescoes and bronzes, prehistoric flints and Islamic bookbindings, note the mosaics (one of wrestlers, striking), the funerary bric-à-brac (a crudely painted 3rd-century bull-fight from Thaenae), the jewellery (from the basilica of La Skhira) and the Roman glass (wine-jugs in the shape of snails and a *rhyton* or drinking vessel).

Sfax Medina From the Place Hedi Chaker the Boulevard de la République runs broad and well-shaded on to the **Bab ed-Divan**. The original 1306 passageway in this 'Council Gate', to the left of its three 1944 additions, makes a worthy start to a medina almost as charming as Tunis'. (Reputedly accessible to Christians only since 1832, it now has signs and notices aplenty to aid the infidels.) Behind the food and handicraft shops in the gateway, the Rue des Andalous climbs past the Mosque of Sidi Abdul-Mulla to the Rue Mongi Slim, the main street of the medina (where the disciplined Sfaxis all keep to the right). Follow the signs (right) to the **Museum of Popular Arts and Traditions**, installed in the Dar Jellouli (early 18th-century, renovated 1728). The galleries of this Andalusian palace are worth seeing as are its collections of costumes, arms and cosmetics, interiors, furniture and household implements. A 'provisions room' contains huge oil *jarres* and a culinarily useful case of herbs and spices transcribed in French and Arabic. Upstairs exhibits are *costumes feminins de Sfax*. Beside displays of Arab calligraphy are some of the finest examples to be found of Tunisian painting on glass. The **Rue Mongi Slim** continues through a warren of workshops and suqs – the **Souk el Jemaa**, left in the Rue des Aghlabites, selling spices, herbs, gum-arabic and chameleons, dead in polythene bags, to ward off the Evil Eye. Narrow stairs climb between the stalls to an upper-storey world of workshops. The covered suqs, off left behind the Mosque of Sidi Mseddi, are slightly disappointing.

Accommodation

Doyen of the old-time hotels is **Les Oliviers**, 3-star (tel: 04 25 188), a 'French provincial' mansion from 1923 renovated in 1969. More modern are **Le Colisée**, 2-star (tel: 04 27 800), the **Mondial**, 2-star (tel: 04 26 620), and the **Thyna**, 2-star (tel: 04 25 266). Newest and best are the excellent **Syphax**, 4-star (tel: 04 43 333), a modestly elegant Novotel nearest the airport, and the **Sfax Centre**, 4-star luxe (tel: 04 25 700).

One of the best preserved of its kind, El Jem's amphitheatre is said to have seated up to 30,000

A long-suffering donkey accepts its load on the beach of El Attaya, Kerkenna Islands

◆◆
KERKENNA ISLANDS (ÎLES KERKENAH)

An hour or so by ferry from the hectic city of Sfax brings you to this idyllic backwater. A Society for the Exploitation of the Islands of Kerkenna was founded in 1961 to ensure that Tourism with a capital T would take off. As it has still not taken off (thank goodness), the islanders are now pinning their hopes on Sfax's new international airport. The Greeks as early as the 5th century BC knew the islands as *Kyrannis* (where Hannibal sought refuge in 195 BC). Caesar sent troops to the Roman *Cercina* to seize the Pompeians' supplies, and in AD 15 one Caius Sempronius Gracchus was exiled to Kerkenna and executed – for seducing the emperor's daughter. Both subsequent invasions by Byzantines, Arabs and Normans, and lack of water and work – just sponges, dates, alfa and olives, a few vines, figs, sheep and fish – explain the mass migration to the mainland (where nowadays you find the menfolk employed as waiters and restaurateurs). **Mellita** is one name of the first island and its 'capital'; another is Gharbi (the 'Western') and, following a Roman causeway, a

serviceable road links this with Chergui, the 'Eastern' island. Opposite the *fsaqia* of Ouled Yaneg, the *zone touristique* is copiously signposted.
Shaking off Ouled Kacem's clinging white cottages, the main road crosses Ouled Bou Ali. **Remla**, with the only petrol station, is *ipso facto* the island's capital and, after Kellabine, Abbassia boasts its only **Roman ruins** – only vestigial house-walls, trenches and one black-and-white mosaic survive from antique *Abbassia*.
The road – and the efficient 'Soretras' bus service – ends in the delta of lanes that filter through El Attaya. Better turn off to the left before it, by the causeway marked *Résidence du Salut du Prent Bourguiba*. This '**Place of Safety**' is the historic *loud* fishing-boat by which Bourguiba, fleeing the French, escaped from Sfax on 27 March 1945, the shack in which he hid for three days before leaving for Libya, and the fascinating gallery of 'freedom fighter' photographs.

Access
By ferry from Sfax, 60–70 minutes. Telephone 04 22 216 for details of passenger and car ferries (up to six daily).

Accommodation
The **Grand**, 2-star (tel: 04 81 266), is an amazing rarity nowadays: a seafront hotel where from your room you hear not air conditioners, lifts, discos or traffic but . . . the sea. The adjacent **Farhat**, 2-star (tel: 04 81 236), is angular blocks slightly Aztec in style, and the **Résidence Club Holiday Village** (tel: 04 81 221) is unblushingly for the youthful or frugal.

◆◆◆ KAIROUAN ✓

Kairouan is Tunisia's 'holy city' (the Islamic duty of a pilgrimage to Mecca being redeemable by visiting Kairouan seven times, or four, say some, or even nine). As with Lourdes, Rome and Jerusalem, the pursuit of religion goes hand in hand with good business sense, Kairouanis being the country's sharpest carpet manufacturers and salesmen, and the first to develop hotels in Hammamet. The Muslim conquerors, on their third incursion in AD668, chose this site for their capital. It lay on important caravan routes (*Kairouan* meaning 'caravan' and not, as everyone will tell you, 'fortified place'); it was equidistant from their coastal enemies, the Byzantines, and those in the hills, the Berbers and, according to legend, as the leader Oqba ibn Nafi arrived, there opened at his feet a spring in which he found a gold cup lost years before in Mecca. This clinched the spot's sanctity. Kairouan enjoyed a heyday as national capital: the Aghlabites developed a reportedly sumptuous city, which the Beni Hilal laid low in 1057.

Watch for street names in **Kairouan** which change frequently, causing confusion for many vistors.

Carpet-making in Kairouan, a traditional and highly valued craft

With the Great Mosque's minaret distinctive above the encircling greenery as you approach from Tunis or Sousse, the road forks round the city walls. Off right, to the north of the city, are the shrines of Sidi Naji, Sidi Ali el Obeidi, Sidi Saleh, Sidi El Harbawi and Sidi Yusef Dahmani. Beyond their marabouts lie the 9th-century **Aghlabite Pools**: one large and one small, restored to their (putatively) pristine state; two others excavated to the east; several more suspected round about. At their entrance stands the smart ticket office where all

visitors must purchase passes to enter Kairouan's mosques, after filling out an authorisation form undertaking to behave correctly in the holy places. This ticket office is open from 08.00–17.00hrs. The 'ring-road' leads westward to the 'Mausolée de la Mosquée du Barbier', the **Zawia of Sidi Sahib**. Situated opposite the Martyrs' Memorial, with a 1629 cupola and a 1690 minaret, the shrine is an attractive complex of patios, corridors and 'cells' for the *medersa* pupils. In the final patio, looking splendid with ceramic-tiled and sculpted-plaster walls, Sidi Sahib's tomb is draped in white and green, adorned with prints of Mecca and usually screened by a cluster of white-clad women. Its 7th-century incumbent (really Abu Jama'el Balawi) was called Sidi Sahib (the Companion) because of his association with the Prophet Mohammed. The *zawia* itself is called the 'Barber's Mosque' because Abu Jama' possessed three hairs of the Prophet's beard.

Opposite the Aghlabite Pools, the Rue Ibn Jazzar rises past the crenellated **kasba** to meet the medina at the Porte de Tunis. Refaced and repointed, the **walls** belie their 900 years (although the 1052 structure was repaired in 1712 – and breached again when the Axis troops needed rock for their landing-strip).

Behind the Tunis Gate's three entrances, ornate with arcades, columns and inscriptions, the brothel lies immediately right. So look discreetly left: the minaret of the Sidi Bou Misra Mosque is neatly restored and re-inscribed with the password of Islam: 'There is no god but God'. The main street, renamed **Avenue Habib Bourguiba** after that ex-president's conciliatory visit in 1969, dissects the **medina** ahead. *Attarine* (perfumers), *Sekkajin* (saddlers), *Leffa* (cloth), the suqs are colourful beside their Tunis counterparts.

Follow the Avenue Habib Bourguiba on. Sharp left after the first 'pergola', the restored 17th-century **Bir Barouta** offers the odd spectacle of a camel in an upstairs room turning a wheel to raise water from a well that some Muslims believe connects with Mecca. To judge by the taste, it travels well. The next alley left after the next pergola leads to the **Zawia of Sidi Abid el Ghariani**, the 14th-century shrine of one Abu Samir Abid bin Ya'ish el Ghariani, a native Libyan who studied and taught here.

Behind the **Bab es-Shuhada** ahead (the Martyrs' Gate) is the Place de l'Indépendance. To the left beside the walls stands the post-war Negra Mosque, in the walls the **Bab el Jedid** (Newgate), the gate of Monqas ben Rejeb and the now-closed Bab et-Tkia.

Through a fourth gate, the **Bab el Khukha** (1705), a lane of white walls, blue doors and black lamp-brackets leads to the **Great Mosque** (open 09.00 to 14.00hrs except during prayer times). Oqba ibn Nafi's original edifice was re-built in 695, extended in 743, replaced in 774 and again, finally, in 836,

when Ziyadat-Allah raised the whole plot some 10 feet (3m). His Aghlabite structure was renovated thoroughly in 1025, 1294, 1618 and in 1970-2 (for the town's 1,300th anniversary). It is not only one of the most historically hybrid mosques in Africa, it is also the oldest and most revered.

The *midha* (ablutions room) may or may not be a museum again but, facing the mosque's west wall, it marks the entrance to the colonnaded courtyard. In the paving, seven wells have rims furrowed by generations of bucket-ropes; another is patterned in horseshoe cavities said to be for the hooves of animals drinking: really there to decant the rainwater. To the southeast is the façade of the prayer-room. Its 'forest of columns' is perhaps a cliché but no other description is adequate: columns from Roman Carthage and Sousse; some Byzantine, some Aghlabite; columns inscribed with Christian crosses; columns you must squeeze between if you are not to be judged too fat for Paradise; columns in marble, three even in porphyry (given, so they say, by Charlemagne in return for Saint Cyprian's remains). Their capitals are Roman, Byzantine or Arab – since 1970 some are Tunisian too. In the doors and ceiling you could still see some of the 1,100-year-old wood, were the prayer-room not out of bounds to tourists. (As compensation, your ticket includes entry to the Barber's Mosque, Sidi el Ghariani's and the Aghlabite Pools).

Dominating the court is the

plain, squat and unique minaret (dated 836; 114-foot/35m high; Christian fish sculpted in some of its 128 steps and a fine but now forbidden view from the summit).

Accommodation

Much of a muchness at **Les Aghlabites**, 3-star (tel: 07 20 855) and the **Continental**, 4-star (tel: 07 21 135), with 'olde-worlde' walls and portal which is opposite the Aghlabite Pools. But the **Splendid**, 3-star (tel: 07 20 522), has more character. It is situated in a 'French colonial' corner-block on a quiet central square beside the police.

Festival

The old town is decked with flags and fairy-lights for the annual festival of Mouled, the Prophet Mohammed's birthday (a movable feast as arbitrary as Christmas and ignored by strict Muslims elsewhere).

◆◆
SBEÏTLA

Here, where the first Muslim raid of AD 647 turned back, are the ruins of Roman *Sufetula*. Mentioned only in later lists of bishoprics, Sufetula is documented by its monuments and inscriptions alone. Of the latter, the earliest dates from Vespasian (AD 69–79). Start, to the right of the road, with Diocletian's **triumphal arch** (c.290). Prosperity under the Roman empire is attested by olive-presses, three vestigial **thermae** (baths) and the **theatre**, prettily sited beside the *oued* with its orchestra paving

and some seats remaining; by the unexcavated but distinctively shaped **amphitheatre** (nearest the hotel) and above all by the famous temples of the **forum**. In the absence of inscriptions we can only assume that, as at Dougga, these were dedicated in the 2nd century AD to Jupiter, Juno and Minerva. Byzantine walling encumbers them and, opposite the **museum** at the entrance, three fortresses are further relics of this 6th–7th-century seat of the patrician-bishops and Tunisia's ephemeral capital. But Sufetula's distinction is its 4th- and 5th-century churches. North of the three temples, the **Church of Vitalis** is identified by the beautiful white 'upholstery' of its baptismal font – and by the saint's name in crude mosaic. The nearby **Church of Bellator** has a similarly curvaceous baptistry, the body of the kirk being a square colonnade. The Vandals conducted worship here too: the **Church of Servus** (near the theatre) they converted from a pagan temple into a Donatist chapel and, between the churches of Vitalis and Bellator, a house was adapted as the tomb of St Jucundus, a Catholic who was martyred by the fellow-Christian Vandals.

Accommodation

Better than the **Bakini**, 2-star (tel: 07 65 244), beside the main road in, the **Sufetula**, 2-star (tel: 07 65 074), dominates the Roman ruins of the same name, with a panorama of antiquity from your bedroom window.

JERBA AND THE SOUTH

♦♦♦

JERBA

If the island of Jerba is usually tagged on to the end of books about Tunisia, it is not only because it lies like a geographical afterthought down by the Libyan border. Idyllic but detached, Jerba is also an outsider in politics, religion and population.

Our knowledge of Jerba begins in myth. Ulysses, sailing from Troy, reached a desert island where the people lived blissfully on lotus. No one knows what the lotus-drink was. *Cordia myxa*, say some; crab-apple cider, say others, or *lâghmi*, palm-wine. Jerba, Mallorca, Menorca and Malta all claim to identify with 'Lotus-land': so Jerba, for extra legend-cover, also believes itself to be Ogygia, where Calypso held Ulysses captive. History starts with the Romans, who built *Girba*, *Haribus*, *Meninx* and *Tipasa*, perhaps on Phoenician foundations. Jerba's contribution to the classical era is appropriately small-scale; the emperors Gallus and Valerianus were born here – to reign a joint total of nine years (AD 251-60). Vandals, Byzantines and Hilalians found little to destroy, but the island's useful anchorage on a flat,

For centuries, fishing has been one of Jerba's main forms of employment: it still provides an important source of income

JERBA AND THE SOUTH

sandy coast attracted the medieval sea powers. Roger II, that piecemeal empire-builder who ruled Sicily, Prussia and Jerusalem, took it in 1134. Its conquerors thereafter read like a list of prize-winners: Roger de Loria 1284, Raymond Montaner 1331, the Moroccan Merinites 1335, Pedro Navarro 1510, Charles V 1535. The sieges and slaughters reached a climax in 1560 when the Pope's French, Spanish and Neapolitan troops joined forces with the Knights of Malta to crush once and for all the pirate lair that Dragut had made of Jerba . . . only 5–6,000 Christians survived the first encounter in May and fled to the Borj el Kebir. On 31 July Dragut evicted and massacred them, piling their skulls on the beach. There was some resistance to the French army in 1881 but World Wars I and II passed Jerba by.

Throughout all this the Jerbans continued to grow olives and palms, weave carpets, and fish. They were also inbreeding to a distinctive type – short, long-headed and sallow-skinned. This perhaps lies behind their present feeling of detachment. In religion, too, there is isolation. The Jerbans welcomed the 7th-century Muslim invaders, then turned to an unorthodox sect of Islam: as Kharijites still, they are Muslim Quakers, slightly austere, egalitarian and mild-mannered, believing in conscience as a rule of conduct. But nature more than religion has dictated their recent history. Lack of water had always limited progress and, in the last two centuries, has led to mass emigration.

The island measures 18 by 17½ miles (29 by 28km) at its longest and widest; the generally blissful beaches extend for almost 80 miles (128km) and the highest point above sea-level is all of 182 feet (55m). Exports are primarily carpets but also fish, sponges, pottery and soap. Of the 213 mosques all are different and most unique, minor wonders so coated and recoated with whitewash and plaster that they seem to have melted and set again off-centre.

All of this, however, is of no more than academic interest as you lie in the sun (average 344 days annually) or swim in the shallow seas (average 68°F/20°C). If you should want to see what else the island offers, you can do so in a day. Hotels have excursions or hire cars, mobilettes and bicycles. The roads are modestly good, but narrow and winding and quite justifying the island's speed limit of 44 miles/70km per hour. Unlikely to exceed that, camels and horses wait at most hotel entrances, ready for your ride.

For the island's 'capital', **Houmt Souk**, see pages 73–5.

The island's beach hotels stretch along the shores of Sidi Mahrez and La Seguia, the *zone touristique* to the west and south respectively of the northeastern Ras Tourguemess. The nearest source of local colour to these beach hotels is **Midoun**, almost

Clay for the potteries of Guellala is dug out of the nearby hillsides

a village. Here the main Place Meninx of standard souvenir displays fronts the arched fruit and meat market and a brand-new 'Old Town'. The Great Mosque borders the Aghir road, and the market is on Fridays.

From Midoun good roads run either via Aghir ('*Centre de Camping*') or Mahboubine (with the main-square Mosque of El Katib, 'the Clerk', 1902–3), to **El Kantara**. This causeway, which leads to Zarsis, is a winding freak of a thoroughfare, 32 feet (9.75m) wide and 4 miles (6.5km) long. It had Roman and perhaps Phoenician precursors; in 1515 Dragut pierced it to escape

with his fleet from Andrea Doria's naval blockade. Northwest along the coast from El Kantara, the hamlet of **Guellala** lies scattered over hills of palms and well-heads, its kilns smoking ceaselessly beside the high piles of pots. These are the standard coarse *gargoulettes* but the shops, now businesslike to left and right, sell other delightful objects as well as cheap and ingenious 'terracotta tricks'.

A 7-mile (11km) road climbs gently inland to Er-Riadh ('the Gardens'), once called **Hara Seghira** ('Little Ghetto'). Here the **Ghriba** is a synagogue famed throughout the Middle East and centre of an international pilgrimage each Passover. Even writers insisting on the Israelites'

JERBA AND THE SOUTH

Baskets for sale in Houmt Souk

arrival in AD 70 accept that the Ghriba was founded '600 years before Christ'. A holy stone fell from heaven to mark the site and a mysterious foreign girl – a *ghriba* – appeared, helped the builders with miracles and gave the place its name. The present building dates from 1920. Beyond the arch you see the Pilgrims' Hostel and, opposite, the wooden doors through which, having covered your head, you may visit an interior unique rather than inspirational.

From Er-Riadh a road runs to Houmt Souk via **Hara Kebira**. The name ('Big Ghetto' or 'Quarter') is equally as self-explanatory. How and when the Hebrew community came to Jerba is not known.

The Jews themselves date their presence here from the Babylonian Captivity in 590 BC; historians opt for Titus' destruction of the Temple in AD 70; the only evidence is the 10th-century tomb of one Cohen. Certain is the Jerban Jews' racial purity – obvious from their features – and their decline. Of the 5,000 resident in 1956, some 750 and 290 now remain in Hara Kebira and Hara Seghira respectively.

Accommodation

The only 5-star is Hasdrubal (tel: 05 57 650). **El Menzel**, 4-star (tel: 05 57 070), a suave white delight that for many connoisseurs alone justifies a return to Jerba. The **Abou Nawas**, 4-star (tel: 05 57 022), and **Palm Beach**, 4-star (tel: 05 57 350), are twins with the same-named hotels in Hammamet. The **Ulysse Palace**, 4-star (tel: 05 57 482), was renovated in 1990. The **Dar Jerba**, 3/2-star (tel: 05 57 191), does for the traditional hotels what hypermarkets do for the village store: a single complex 880 yards (800m) long that links 4 hotels, 4 pools, 10 restaurants, 6 bars and (at the last count) 2,650 beds. The 3-star options are the older **Les Sirènes** (tel: 05 57 266) and **El Bousten** (tel: 05 57 200), but accommodation is as good in the **El Jazira**, 2-star (tel: 05 57 300), the **Médina**, 2-star (tel: 05 57 233), the **Pénélope**, 2-star (tel: 05 57 055) and **Tanit**, 2-star (tel: 05 57 132). The last is super-Jerban beside a lagoon on the island's tip. The **Sidi Slim**,

2-star (tel: 05 57 021/3), also caters for campers in the adjoining 'Sidi Ali Club'. The **Club Méditerranée** is stylish at Jerba la Douce, simple at Jerba la Fidèle, but both are bookable only beforehand in Europe.

For Houmt Souk hotels, see under **Houmt Souk**, below.

Festivals

There is a traditional Ulysses Festival, *Festival de l'Île de Djerba*, in July. During the November–December olive harvest, the islanders all seem to be either up or under trees, picking olives.

Shopping

Hotel boutiques and Houmt Souk shops carry all the standard lines in leather, pottery, olive-wood and brass but, thanks to Hara Kebira's Jewish jewellers, gold and silver are a speciality in the suqs of Houmt Souk (where the amount of 'antique work' is amazing).

◆◆

HOUMT SOUK, JERBA

The islanders of Jerba traditionally live not grouped in towns or villages, but isolated in scattered family homesteads called *menzels*. For this reason Houmt Souk is the only real conurbation and, for that reason, the island's capital.

The **Museum of Popular Arts and Traditions** occupies the Zawia (Shrine) of Sidi Zituni northeast of the town, and has exhibits well displayed and labelled (although this is in French and sometimes only in Arabic), of local costumes, jewellery (in an exquisite 'honeycomb' cupola), household implements and pottery (including the 66-gallon/300-litre *duh*), a mock-potter's workshop in the former cistern below, and coffers – carved, painted and studded abundantly – for clothes and/or coffins. *Open*: summer: 08.00–12.00hrs, 15.00–19.00hrs; winter: 08.30–16.30hrs.

Turning right as you leave the museum, you can keep straight on to the **Mosque of the Turks** (*Jami' et-Turuk*), interesting outside only with its phallic minaret and bath-house dome. Or fork left to the Place Sidi Brahim Jemni. Opposite, in the **Strangers' Mosque**, the interior is a masterpiece of simplicity while the exterior is curious, with its main dome surrounded apparently by offspring. It is closed to non-Moslems. Continuing along the beach, you pass the Regional Tourist Office and come to the **Borj el Kebir**, the Great Tower. A Roman statue found in recent excavations indicates the site's first occupants. Roger de Loria, given Jerba in 1284 as the King of Aragon's reward for taking it, built a first fort. This the Hafsite sultan Abu Faris razed when, in the early 15th century, he built the present edifice to help the islanders withstand Spanish attacks.

Next along the beach backed by the 1-star hotel Dar Faïza and the Lotos, a simple pyramid commemorates the

Tower of Skulls. Dragut's macabre anti-Christian trophy stood here from 1560 until 1848, when the European colony prevailed upon the bey to have it removed to the Christian cemetery.

From here double back into town via the Avenue Habib Bourguiba. Off left, only a Great War plinth to the '*Soldats Français de Djerba*' survives of the unholy shambles that was the Christian cemetery. Fork right between the ONA store and the **Shaikh's Mosque** (which was recently literally straightened up, so that steps and uprights are no longer quaintly off true) to reach the main square from which the name Houmt Souk (Market Quarter) derives.

Backing the main square, the Place Bechir Seoud is all touristic souvenir shops (a façade for the daily victuals market behind). It leads to the Place Farhat Hached, where begin the **suqs**, closer and homelier than those of Tunis and colourful with clothes, shoes, silks, brass, silver and leatherware. Next comes the Place Moktar Attia along with its cafés, banks, chemists and arcaded Souvenir de l'Île store. This in turn gives on to the Place Hedi Chaker's small cheap eating-places.

Straight on past the Baccar, Bluemoon and Méditerranéen restaurants, the Rue Moncef Bey narrows through the arcade of the Tunisian Touring Club's Marhala Hotel. The island's only cinema then indicates the lane that leads to the twin-spired **church** (now a private keep-fit club) and to the Arischa Hotel.

Leaving the Place Hedi Chaker between the restaurants de l'Île, Neptune and du Sud, you find yourself back on the Place Sidi Brahim Jemni (above) where, beside the 'Bain Turk', that worthy's *zawia* is now the taxi-drivers' office (built 1674; tel: 05 50 205).

Accommodation

If you really cannot reach a beach hotel, the **Hajji**, 1-star (tel: 05 50 630), is better than the **Nozha**, 1-star (tel: 05 50 381). For cheaper accommodation with more

Over 300,000 palms flourish in the lush Gabes oasis, which centres on Chenini and boasts a Roman dam (see page 77)

character, try the nearby
Arischa (tel: 05 50 384) or
Marhala (tel: 05 50 146) – both
offsetting their no-star rating
with a quaint hippy-kibbutz
atmosphere.

Restaurants
Commendable dishes in the
restaurants mentioned above
(page 74) are delicious, cheap
and principally fish.

◆◆
ZARZIS
Spelt in Arabic 'Jarjis' and
mispronounced, Zarzis is a
French-protectorate creation on
the site of Roman *Gergis*. It is
the market-town of a region that
was, until the 1950s, thought to
be barren nomads' land. The
French experiment in
rehabilitating the Accara

Beduin to settle and tend
olive-groves on soil considered
uncultivable succeeded against
all expectation.

The area's other established
asset is its long shore of villas
and hotels. As you come in from
Jerba, a first signpost sends you
seaward to **Oamarit**, an
apparently placeless name, past
the cliff road (left) then to the
Oamarit hotel complex and the
adjacent Sangho Club Hotel. A
second turning (left) then joins
the first to loop along the
seafront of palms, bitty farming,
homesteads and mosques
that precede the hotels Zita,
Zarzis and Zéphir. From their
camp-following of bazaars and
souvenir booths, police, Le
Pacha Restaurant and Tourist
Office, the road climbs the
hillside to rejoin the main road
into town.

Zarzis simply relaxes round its
cross-roads. It does not, *pace*
the guide-books, have a Turkish
fort opposite the Delegation this
was obliterated to make way for
the Great Mosque in 1978. The
latter's minaret – and the Big
Brother mast – loom over the
town centre, which banks and
administrative blocks, a
supermarket, small **museum**,
ONA store and Les Palmiers
Restaurant all help update. The
market takes place each
Monday and Friday morning.

Accommodation
The **Zita**, 2-star (tel: 05 80 346),
is the oldest: simple, far-flung
but sufficiently successful to
have funded the construction of
the next-door **Zarzis**, 3-star (tel:
05 80 160). The township's best,
with a magnificent sweep of

Carriage rides are a popular tourist attraction in Gabes, as well as a handy way to explore the gardens of the oasis

brick-vaulted hall, this has likewise enabled the owners to acquire the hotel next door, the **Zéphir**, 2-star (tel: 05 81 026). On the crumbling bluff of Oamarit, the **Oamarit**, 3-star (tel: 05 80 770), and the adjacent **Sangho Club Hotel**, 3-star (tel: 05 80 124), are sporty, relaxed and well equipped.

◆◆
MEDENINE

Medenine, where the Eighth Army paused before storming the Mareth Line in 1943, and which British Government papers described as a village in 1945, later became the county-town of the largest Tunisian governorate – and is still little more than a village. A wide *oued* (or valley) divides it (*Medenine* meaning 'Two Towns'). The southern slope is uninteresting with its administrative buildings, the unclassified Sahara Hotel and a signpost reading 'Cairo 2606'. Quainter are the roads that rise in a trident up the opposite slope: between them the significantly named **Place de l'Évacuation** and left of the Rue des Palmiers, the lower road to Jorf, the square *ksar* of *ghorfas*. The **ghorfas** are the most striking of the Berbers' varied dwellings. Like narrower, higher Roman cisterns or small Nissen huts, these rock and mud vaults are built one against the other, one above the other, in long terraces up to six storeys high (although Medenine's have nearly all collapsed). Interiors are approximately 30 feet (9m) long, 10 feet (3m) wide and 6 feet (1.8m) high. Stone steps climb outside, or inside through holes in the ceiling, to upper storeys.

Designed as safe storage for the nomads' produce, some *ghorfas* were on occasions inhabited (despite what government guides maintain – the Arabic word after all means 'room').

FOUM TATAOUINE

Market and administrative centre for the nearby mountains of the Ksour, Foum Tataouine does its best to look older than its three score years and ten.

Antiquated arches surround the marketplace Ali Belhaouane, picturesque each Monday and Thursday morning with its (all-male) market (burnuses, kashabias, Berber rugs and blankets; alfa mats, baskets and – sometimes – beduin silver; seeds, dates or peppers according to the season, and joss-sticks to offset the smell of dried fish). Fragments of Roman masonry, all from elsewhere, look lost on the hillside below the old Governorate; but especially on a hot dusty summer's day, the township still feels like the convict settlement it was established as in 1912, and you appreciate even the Hôtel La Gazelle.

Accommodation
Transformed by the 3-star **Hotel Sangho**, 3km out of town on a hillside. In town is **La Gazelle**, 2-star (tel: 06 60 009).

CHENINI

This is the best known of the fascinating Berber fastnesses that picket the Ksour, the barren mountains south of Foum Tataouine.

In a magnificent gorge of tumbled boulders, Chenini's steep antique honeycomb of cliff homes rises to a peak between the old and new Great Mosques. You can only wonder at the fear or xenophobia that drove men to make these crags their homes – so high that there is no longer grazing for their flocks, so steep that sometimes two people cannot pass on the narrow ledge 'streets'.

Access
Found 12 miles (19km) west of Foum Tataouine, the place is best reached by the turning signposted (right) off the GP 19 south.

Accommodation
La Gazelle in Foum Tataouine or, more quaintly, in the *ghorfa* hotel at **Ksar Haddada**, due north from Chenini by a new 12-mile (19km) road, or via Ghoumrassen (tel: 05 69 605).

Restaurants
By the roadhead, below the new Great Mosque, the **Relais Chenini Hotel Bar-Restaurant** is a pricey hole in the rock (with no rooms).

GABES (GABÈS)

The last passable watering-place on the road south before Jerba and the Libyan border, the town of Gabes is not unattractive. But its seaside oasis is unforgettable. It may seem odd to travel to Africa, then drive miles in order to walk through a market-garden. But Gabes' gardens are unlike any other: 4 square miles (10sq km) behind the coast, more than 300,000 palms – and from the Ras el Oued (the Head of the Valley) you can overlook them entirely. The word 'overlook' is usefully ambiguous, for the oasis starts deep in the canyonlike Oued Gabes. Look down and the valley floor is delightful with palms, fruit-trees and rushes mirrored in the waters. Take a step or two backwards and the oasis disappears, the desert plateau stretching away before you, apparently unbroken.

The town's history is not fully known. Perhaps a Punic trading station preceded the Roman colony of *Tacapae;* perhaps Berbers and Byzantines settled here before Sidi Boulbaba, the Prophet's barber, built the first mosque in the 680s. What Arabs, Spanish and Turks may have left behind vanished, just like much of the French-protectorate town, first in the bombardments of 1943 then in the floods of 1962.

From the main road's youth hostel and ONA workshop ('Tunisish Hand Craft Office'), the Avenue Farhat Hached cuts through town past the daily market to the **Place de la Libération**. The Martyrs' Garden and obelisk adorn this triangular main square. The Tourist Office (tel: 05 70 254) is likewise triangular on the Avenue Habib Thameur, which meets the beach half a mile (1km) further. Right, the Oasis and Chems hotels; ahead, the

Casino (café-restaurant); left, the stumpy esplanade, lighthouse and blockhouse of the still-expanding port.

The track that, opposite the main-road Agil station, runs over the *oued* and into the **oasis** had by 1972 become such a tourist thoroughfare that it was bituminised, so drivers no longer run the risk of getting lost. Alternatively you can take a bus or taxi, or even hire a horse-carriage. Between dense palms and high frond fences the delightful lane winds to Chenini (2 miles/3km). You might then welcome the 'Cascade' more for its cold drinks than its now-waterless waterfall, before bearing right, as you meet the broad *oued*, to the **Roman dam** (3 miles/4.5km). This once-peaceful corner of antique cultivation is now hard-pressed by souvenir booths, unsightly with pylons and a noisy pumphouse – and exploited by the **crocodile farm** and **zoo**. The walk up through the orchards to the Chela Club and the two higher dams (one Roman, one 1895) is not far – and so charming that you would not notice if it were. The drive on and the fork back bring you past the classic bird's-eye view from the cliffs (4 miles/6km).

Accommodation
Beside the sea, the **Chems**, 2-star (tel: 05 70 547), or, without pool, the adjoining **Oasis**, 3-star (tel: 05 70 381). Inland, the **Néjib**, 2-star (tel: 05 71 686), is surprisingly quiet for a town-centre location, the

Chela Club even more so, set in the upper reaches of the Ras el Oued canyon (tel: 05 24 466).

Shopping

Beside the southbound road into Gabes, and around the Jara quarter there, booths sell chairs, tables and baskets (for infants and/or dogs) made of plaited palm-fronds. They are reasonable and original but, like cheap clothes, tend to lose their shape with use.

♦♦♦
MATMATA ✓

From Gabes, the road south to Matmata cuts inland across the undulating Plain of Arad and rises into the Mountains of Matmata: some are peaks of 2,000 feet (600m) but most are bald buff domes and eroded gulches, with in every hollow a palm-tree or two and a patch of cultivation. Then there is the

village of Tijma and a steep, twisting climb before you bend to a view of the Matmata Valley. Modern white homes and mosques rather mar the surface-of-the-moon effect that travellers once described. The scene is, none the less, somehow unreal: a broad saucer of raw earth, which is spiked with palms and pock-marked with the craters of some 700 pits, dug by the Matmata Berbers who, like the Bulla Regia Romans, found underground homes the best defence against summer heat. The pits are circular and about 30 feet (9m) in both depth and diameter. An entrance tunnel starts some distance away – to allow a gentle slope – and usually has chambers off for the animals. In the walls of the *haush* (the courtyard) are the remarkably snug rooms, 20 feet (6m) long, well insulated but

Carpet weavers at work in the National Handicraft Office, Gabes

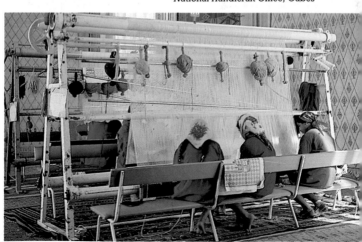

inclined to collapse if rain loosens the soil. Spikes in the walls, or a knotted rope, help you to the next 'floor'. Housewives, gorgeous in red and blue *futas* and black *bakhnugs*, still grind corn or couscous in millstones used since time immemorial. But with rising living standards in recent years, their families' living quarters have also literally risen – to the new street-level settlement where, to a man, the inhabitants have surfaced from their subterranean world.

Accommodation

There is now a modern 3-star, the Troglodyte (tel: 05 30 088). In the 1960s the Tunisian Touring Club converted a basic set of pits for visitors to stay in: the **Marhala** (tel: 05 30 015) has 100 beds in 36 'cells' for parties of 2–10. The **Sidi Driss** 'Hotel' (tel: 05 30 005) is newer, and proud of having served in 1976 as base for the makers of the film *Star Wars*. The newest, **Les Berbères** (tel: 05 30 024), has 7 restaurants and 80 beds in 35 'cells'.

KEBILI

A last-minute halt for travellers to Douz and the 'Sahara safari', Kebili was made a governorate in 1981 and has consequently mushroomed from a (Tuesday) market-village to a desert county-town. Recently renamed the **Museum of National Liberation**, the *Dar* ('House of') *Bourguiba* was, from 3 September until 2 October 1934, a penal stop-over in which the (then future and now

ousted) president was held *en route* for the French penitentiary at Borj Leboeuf. The nearby main square is lively with cafés, police and post office.

Accommodation

Off in the oasis, the **Fort des Autriches**, 2-star (tel: 05 90 233), originally a barracks, then an ostrich farm, has been refurbished and is equipped with a swimming pool.

DOUZ

The desultory settlement of Douz, centre for the nomadic Mrazig tribe, used to wake only weekly for the picturesque Thursday market. But latterly it has responded to tourism with new hotels including the Saharien, Toouareg, Les Roses de Sable and Mehari, and the **Festival du Sahara**, three mid-winter days (which vary each year) of camel parades, races and fights, lectures and local dances, displays of beduin crafts, paintings and photographs. Coach parties limit their T E Lawrence aspirations to the 'Rentacamel' service from the Information Bureau. (Telephone 05 95 341/351 for any number of the 150 mounts and camelteers on call: a 90-minute ride, with optional hire of Arab costume.) Past bitty farms, the camels plod onto the first dunes of this Great Eastern Erg – rolling, golden desert, which is best seen at dawn or sunset.

Car drivers can adventure on from Douz to the summer tented camps located at Zafrane, Nouil and Ksar Ghilane.

The brickwork is as attractive as the embroidered rugs and hangings in Tozeur

Accommodation/Restaurants

Les Roses de Sable (tel: 05 95 484), the **Saharien** (tel: 05 95 339) or, by far the best, the **Mehari**, 3-star (tel: 05 95 149), an opulent bastion of desert comfort completed in 1989. In 1993 the 3-star Toouareg (tel: 05 95 285) was opened to rival the Mehari.

◆◆
GAFSA

The county-town of the governorate of the same name, Gafsa is also the region's natural capital. The species of *Homo sapiens* known as Capsian Man takes its name from Roman *Capsa*. Initially a

Berber stronghold, the town was first burned by Marius in his successful campaign of 106 BC against Jugurtha, then under Trajan made a prosperous *colonia* (as is evidenced by the Roman pools and a mosaic found in 1969). The Byzantines renamed it *Justiniana* and evangelised so effectively that, despite the Muslims' capture of its 80,000 inhabitants in 668, the population continued to speak Latin for another 500 years. In 1434 the Hafsites built the **kasba**, which withstood Dragut's siege of 1551 but succumbed in 1556. In 1943 the town changed hands three times, but less damage was done by the fighting than by an explosion in the French arsenal which laid low much of the kasba. The 1963 lawcourt in the Avenue Habib Bourguiba helps fill this breach.

From the end of the Avenue Habib Bourguiba veer left to find the **Roman Pools** – the smaller with just-legible Latin inscriptions above the aperture from which the mineral water used to spout, the larger and more photogenic with the three arches of the **Bey's Palace** as one of the irregular sides, and the two palm-trees and postcard minaret of the **Great Mosque** opposite. The boys are up the trees and diving in before you can manage to pull out a coin.

Accommodation

In town, the **Gafsa**, 2-star (tel: 06 22 676), aspires (but fails) to rival the rebuilt **Maamoun**, 3-star (tel: 06 22 501). For those on a tighter budget somewhere at the cheaper end of the scale is the **Hotel Khalfallah** (tel: 06 21 468), set slightly away from the main hotel area, on Avenue Taieb Mehiri.

Shopping

Gafsa has an ancient reputation for weaving, which you can watch in the ONA workshop, opposite the Martyrs' Memorial on the road to Tozeur.

◆◆

TOZEUR

Tozeur first materialises as a band of green along the *chott*, then as a buff low-lying town

Desert sands meet oasis greenery: deep wells were bored so that 220,000 more palms could grow at the desert township of Nefta

marked only by three minarets. But as you approach you see Tozeur's far more distinctive feature: its brickwork. If, without preconceived ideas, you were asked to imagine the architectural style best suited to this oasis, you might well arrive at what it in fact has: arcades, façades, house-walls and minarets, all of them fashioned in desert-exotic, baked-symmetrical, dusty-ochre brick. The road from Gafsa enters between the youth hostel and police, the turning to Kebili and the **Mosque of Sidi Abid**, a fine example of the brick used monumentally. Ahead at the T-junction of the Avenue Habib Bourguiba, Sidi Owiti shares a meek brick marabout with the Information Office. The Avenue Habib Bourguiba follows past the Firkaus Mosque to the Place Ech-Chabbat: off right, the 'hotel' Essaada; to the left, the daily market, post office and interesting Splendid Hotel. Through the arched and close-bricked alleys of the 14th-century **medina** beyond, the **Archaeological and Traditional Museum** is well marked. It occupies the Zawia of Sidi Ben Issa. The courtyard of worn capitals contains a headless torso of Juba II (Cleopatra's son-in-law), giant pitchers for dates and/or oil, and Roman columns and capitals labelled 'Roman columns and capitals'. Beneath the *qubba* are circumcision costumes and Arabic books, in a side-room muskets and powder-horns, beduin silver, furniture and clothes. Black African statuettes are explained by the presence here of 19th-century slaves. The 'bride's room' is appropriately pretty with silk screens and curtains, cosmetic trinkets and dress.

By the typically bricked Governorate (1981) the main street meets the Avenue Chabbi Abi Elkacem: left to the Grand Hôtel de l'Oasis, further along to the school-complex, the chemist's, the Continental and El Jerid hotels and the palatial 'Tourisme'. The **oasis** is reached, easily on foot, via the lane alongside the Continental Hotel. It winds into the main square of **Bled el Hader**, interesting for its stumpy, Jerid-brick tower on five courses of Roman masonry. The road leads on between groves of palm, banana, fig, henna and pomegranate, past the **Marabout of Sidi Ali bou Lifa** and his venerable jujube-tree *sisyphus spina Christi*. For Paradise, keep to the straight and narrow ahead.

'**Paradise**', predictably now, is a going business concern. The garden that Amor Rehouma took over from his father – *le Créateur du Paradis* – is admittedly a laudable endeavour, but Westerners may find the acre (0.4 hectare) of palms and flowers an overrated 'sight'. There is also a zoological compound.

For a shorter walk and a better panorama, keep straight on past the hotels, the Tourist Office and the shrine of Tozeur's poet, Abul Kacem Chabbi. **Chabia** is distinguished only by its use still of the *johfa*, the silken

howdah borne by a camel in wedding-processions. Take the track marked 'Visitez le Bélvedère' as the road veers right and follow the watercourses on to the **Bélvedère's** cowboy microcosm of eroded rocks and crevasses ('Camping – Thealamenthe' – 'mint tea'). To the right as you enter and leave Tozeur, the arrows indicate Tijani's '**Zoo du Désert**'. At any time of day (or night) you can admire this late snake-catcher's collection of 100-odd specimens. They share the pleasant compound with monkeys, sheep, hyaenas and goats; fennecs, gazelles, deer and caged birds; a Coke-drinking dromedary and two lions, presumed tame behind their low flimsy fence.

Accommodation

The fanciest is the 4-star Abou Nawas Tozeur (tel: 06 52 700). Attractive amidst the brick arches and courtyards of the **Oasis**, 3-star (tel: 06 50 522), far more stylish at the **Ras el Aïn**, 3-star (tel: 06 52 003) and **Hafsi**, 3-star (tel: 06 50 558), youth-hostelish at **El Jerid**, 1-star (tel: 06 50 488), and quaint at the **Splendid**, 1-star (tel: 06 50 053), due to its French-African colonial courtyard and similar mood.

Shopping

Shopping is for several interesting local specialities: stuffed jackals, vipers and lizards, pickled scorpions, palm-frond furniture and local rugs that reproduce in wool the brick-designs of the buildings.

◆◆◆
NEFTA ✓

This striking desert township is the *non plus ultra* for most visitors to Tunisia. As you come in from Tozeur, across undulating desert, it looks to be a similar broad band of green along the distant Chott el Jerid. But what you see here is an artificial oasis made possible by the boring of 2,100 feet (640m) wells in the 1960s.

The simple towns of the Jerid region have developed an attractive style. The people of Tozeur and Nefta have taken the common sand-brick and worked it in bold geometric patterns that make the front of the poorest home an object of interest. That is the architectural style of the arch through which you enter Nefta – and of the roadside Hôtel Le Nomade as well as the magnificent Sahara Palace Hotel (1 mile/1.6km uphill). The hill above the latter is crowned by the **Corbeille**. Beside the Mirage Hotel stands the **Zawia el Qadiria**, with bulbous dome and open minaret; beside that the Corbeille café, and from here you overlook the original **oasis**, with its 152 springs, of Roman *Nepte*. The classic sweep of the buff terraced slopes, topped by domed marabouts and descending to dense palm-groves, is perhaps the loveliest of Tunisia's oasis landscapes. You can explore it on foot or by donkey, but cars are not allowed in.

The enterprising Information Bureau (*Syndicat d'Initiative*) occupies one corner of the Corbeille road below, the Restaurant des Sources the other. After bazaars, banks and governmental buildings – even the police and post office in local brick, the main road dips across the channelled 'natural' oasis. This too is called **Paradis** and you can walk, drive or (best) take a guide from the Syndicat. The enchanting monotony – palms, pomegranates and irrigation channels high on stilts – is broken first by the **Marabout of Sidi Bou Ali** (2 miles/3.5km). Book and candle adorn the tomb of this Moroccan, who planted Nefta's first palm trees in the 13th century. The route opens out to the hospital and the main road, so shy off (sharp right) to the oasis and the old **Great Mosque** (2½ miles/4km). Proceed between old town and oasis and fork right for the Office des Céréales, even its warehouse stylish in local brick, then either left back to the main road (3 miles/5km) or sharp left to the town hall and Martyrs' Memorial on the Place de la Libération. Do not leave Nefta without tasting its famous dates, reputed to be the finest in the region.

Accommodation

The Bel Horizon, completed back in 1992, is a fine 3-star (tel: 06 57 328), and there are two other 3-stars, the Neptus (tel: 06 57 378) and La Rose (tel: 06 57 366).

Situated at the bottom end is the unclassified **Nomade**, (tel: 06 57 052).

The shores of Lake Ichkeul blaze with colourful flowers in spring

PEACE AND QUIET

Wildlife and Countryside in Tunisia
by Paul Sterry

Away from the beaches, Tunisia offers a surprising array of scenery and wildlife. Impressive lakes such as Ichkeul, in the north, attract vast numbers of birds throughout the year and have colourful displays of flowers in spring. Pools and oases are a powerful magnet to resident desert birds and migrants alike and always hold something of interest.

In contrast to the wetlands and lakes, the deserts which cover much of Tunisia have a unique magic of their own. In the south of the country they are sandy and low-lying, but in the north they become quite mountainous. This part of the country forms a geographical extension to the Atlas range which stretches along most of North Africa.

Lake Ichkeul

In a country as arid as Tunisia, water is at a premium. Pools and rivers are often seasonal, drying up in the heat of the summer, so it is not surprising that Lake Ichkeul, a large and permanent water body in the north of the country, attracts vast numbers of birds. Although there are other sizeable lakes in Tunisia, the delicate balance between freshwater from the seasonal, winter rains and the saline influence of the sea in summer has made Ichkeul by far the best in the country and of international importance for its breeding and wintering birds. Situated in the north of the country near the sea at Bizerta, Lake Ichkeul is within easy reach of Tunis and many of the coastal holiday resorts further south. Together with its surrounding marshes, the lake covers an area of over 38 square miles (100sq km) – although the precise dimensions fluctuate markedly according to the seasonal water level.

Lake Ichkeul's backdrop of mountains, which rise to nearly 1,650 feet (500m), provide a superb setting for its birdlife, and in spring this is complemented by the wildflowers of the meadows and agricultural land surrounding the lake. Gladioli, irises and marigolds grow in unbelievable profusion in a sea of reds and yellows, while field borders are full of poppies and many species of the umbellifer or carrot family. In addition to its importance for summer residents and winter visitors, Lake Ichkeul's position on the southern shores of the Mediterranean makes it of importance to migrant birds. In spring and autumn, its shallow margins are thronged with waders such as little stilt, black-winged stilt, spotted redshank and wood sandpiper. Several races of yellow wagtail actively catch insects from the drying mud, while marsh terns, pratincoles, swallows and martins hawk insects in the air above. Freshwater input during the winter months is vital for the maintenance of the

seasonally fluctuating salinity, and without the feeder streams, Lake Ichkeul would gradually become a large saltpan. The freshwater is also important to Tunisia as a developing nation and projects are already under way to dam some of the rivers. Fortunately, a scheme has also been proposed in order to control the lake's salinity with a sluice, so hopefully the long-term future of Ichkeul has been safeguarded.

Lake Ichkeul's Breeding Birds

Spring in Lake Ichkeul sees the arrival of thousands of migrants from south of the Sahara which visit the lake to breed. Their numbers supplement the countless resident birds which spend their entire lives around the lake's margins.

The shallow waters of the lake are always thronged with waders, herons and egrets. Grey herons and little egrets are present all year round, the latter conspicuous with their white plumage and black legs with bright yellow feet. During the summer months, they are joined by cattle egrets, squacco herons and white storks as they pace in search of fish and frogs.

Reedbeds have healthy populations of bitterns which, despite their large size, are seen only rarely. Their booming calls are frequently heard, but the streaked brown plumage provides amazing camouflage as they creep among the dense reeds. Their cryptic marking is enhanced by their habit of 'freezing' motionless when disturbed. During the summer they are joined by little bitterns and graceful purple herons, both of which build platform nests deep in the vegetation.

The reedbeds support vast numbers of Cetti's, great reed and moustached warblers which produce a deafening chorus throughout spring.

Purple Gallinule
The real prize of Lake Ichkeul's reedbeds, however, is the purple gallinule, a dumpy bird somewhat resembling an outsize moorhen. In certain lights, its purple and blue plumage is almost iridescent, and the bright red beak and frontal 'shield' are conspicuous. The quiet observer may see the bird picking its way through the reeds with surprising agility, flicking its tail as it goes. Its progress is greatly assisted by its long, powerful toes, which grasp the reed stems with great precision.

Lake Tunis is another good wetland site that is worth visiting. The lagoon is connected to the Mediterranean and so its waters are saline. As well as gulls, egrets, herons and waders, the lake also attracts flamingos in the winter and cormorants. Lake Tunis lies within the boundaries of the city near the esplanade. Lake Kelbia lies a short distance to the north of Sousse close to route MC48. Herons, egrets, waders and ducks abound and desert birds are sometimes attracted to drink and bathe. Chott el Jerid is a vast, seasonally flooding salt lake which lies adjacent to the road between Kebili and Tozeur. Birdlife depends on the season and level of the lake – flamingos are an irregular highlight of the area – but the wildlife of the surrounding desert is always good. Look for

The purple gallinule is one of Tunisia's most colourful birds. The long toes enable it to walk over lakeside vegetation

PEACE AND QUIET

larks, bustards, wheatears and birds of prey, which can often be seen close to the road.

Lake Ichkeul's Winter Visitors

Just as Ichkeul's summer visitors have begun to embark on the autumn migration across the Sahara to southern Africa, so the lake receives an influx of birds from across the Mediterranean. These visitors from northern Europe have flown south as winter approaches to escape the falling temperatures and impending frosts on their breeding grounds. The mild temperatures and rich waters provide excellent feeding grounds for thousands of

In March and April, swallows arrive from southern Africa

geese, ducks and coots, and although other lakes in Tunisia and northern Africa also attract wintering birds, none can rival Ichkeul for variety of species and numbers.

By comparison with the summer months, winter in Tunisia, as in the rest of the Mediterranean, is a mild and wet season. The rains over the mountains of northern Tunisia bring to life the seasonal rivers, known as *oueds*, which in turn feed the waters of Lake Ichkeul. This annual input of freshwater floods the lake's margins, while at the same time reducing the salinity of the water which has built up during the summer. Fresh growth of aquatic vegetation is encouraged and this provides a feeding ground for over 100,000 wintering waterbirds. Coots are one of the commonest winter visitors to Lake Ichkeul and their loud and distinctive call is a familiar sound. With their all-black plumage and conspicuous white foreheads, they are easy to identify as they dabble and dive in the shallow water in search of pondweeds. Although coots generally feed in large and loose flocks, they are quarrelsome birds and fights often break out between individuals who stray too close to one another.

Huge flocks of wigeon, teal, gadwall and pintail dabble in the muddy shallows and saltmarsh, feeding on vegetation and invertebrates, while pochard favour the deeper waters where they are sometimes accompanied by flocks of flamingos.

Palm doves are confiding birds, often found around towns and villages

Towns and Villages

Although modern resort towns on the coast are not especially attractive to wildlife, in Tunisia's more traditional towns and villages man has a more harmonious relationship with his environment. In the skies over towns and villages throughout Tunisia, parties of common, pallid and alpine swifts scream through the air in search of insects.

Shrubs and bushes in gardens are host to numerous wintering chiffchaffs, and to migrants such as willow and Bonelli's warblers. Resident throughout the year are the common bulbuls that abound wherever shrubby vegetation is encouraged. Bulbuls are a truly African species and make up for their rather sombre appearance with a loud and flute-like song. The more remote towns and villages are often built in the vicinity of water, and even small pools attract interesting wintering and migrant birds like egrets, marbled teal and glossy ibis. Attempts at cultivation are often made where there is enough water to allow basic irrigation

Geckos

Often seen as a movement from the corner of your eye, geckos are common residents in Tunisian houses. With their suckered feet they can walk on walls and ceilings with ease. Tunisians generally tolerate their presence because of the numbers of flies and other unwelcome house guests they consume.

PEACE AND QUIET

and the introduced prickly pear cactus is often used as a field border. Beautifully marked palm doves are abundant and often so confiding that their speckled throats and scaly backs can be seen without the aid of binoculars. Sharing this Spartan agricultural land are agama lizards and the menacing-looking, though harmless, spiny-tailed lizard. Surprisingly even man's rubbish attracts wildlife. Nocturnal visitors to rubbish dumps include foxes, while during the day Egyptian vultures and black kites are often seen. Small numbers of Spanish and desert sparrows are also drawn to these rather unnatural sources of food, the latter being most frequently seen around the desert towns of Dour and Tozeur.

Coasts and Seas

With over 700 miles (1,100km) of coastline, warm seas, blue skies and almost continuous summer sunshine, it is not surprising that tourist resorts are springing up along Tunisia's shores. Despite the localised disturbance that this causes, there are still tranquil beaches and dunes where birds nest and maritime flowers adorn the sands. Rocky headlands around the coast of Tunisia, such as Cap Blanc, are good for watching the passage of seabirds. Cory's and Manx shearwaters sometimes fly by in huge flocks, known as 'rafts', and can be identified by their stiffly held wings. During onshore gales, the lucky observer may even see diminutive storm petrels fluttering between the waves. Although these seabirds may breed on inaccessible cliffs on the mainland of Tunisia, their main colonies are on uninhabited offshore islands

Olives are important both to the economy and the wildlife of Tunisia. Birds nest and feed in the foliage and insects escape the sun's heat

like La Galite. Similarly, the threatened monk seal, although seen occasionally from the mainland, probably breeds offshore.

The yellow-legged race of the herring gull is common and nests on undisturbed ledges. During the winter months, the beaches are often the haunt of visiting waders like redshank, spotted redshank and grey plover, the latter having flown all the way from their breeding grounds in the high Arctic. They are frequently joined by resident Kentish plovers, the most familiar wader of the shores of the Mediterranean region. As they chase along the shore, they look like animated toys running on mechanical legs.

Above the strandline, stocks, spurges and vetches blaze with colour from March until June, sometimes alongside vigorous plants of cottonweed. This plant is so-called for its downy leaves and stems and is almost entirely coastal in its distribution.

Cap Bon, which lies east of Tunis, is another good coastal spot to visit. It is especially good in spring as thousands of birds of prey pass overhead on their way north across the Mediterranean. The south coast of the peninsula has long, sandy beaches, fringed with maritime flowers, while the northern coast has dramatic cliffs. Seabirds can be seen flying past the tip of the headland in strong winds. The wildlife information centre near the village of El Haovaria is worth a visit.

Little Tern
Little terns breed around the coast of Tunisia and prefer sandy or shingle beaches where they are undisturbed. Eggs are laid in a shallow depression called a 'scrape' and consequently they are vulnerable to trampling. Little terns feed by diving into shallow water to catch fish.

Agricultural Land

Thanks to successful irrigation and the planting of hardy, drought-tolerant plants, a surprising area of land in Tunisia is given over to agriculture. Olive groves and orchards of oranges provide important ingredients for the local diet as well as useful cash crops. The wildlife often benefits as well with the trees providing nesting sites for birds, food for a variety of insects and shade from the heat of the sun.

Orphean warblers, summer visitors to Tunisia, sing their scratchy song from the safety of a branch, while that of the resident Sardinian warbler is often delivered in a dancing song-flight. Rufous bushchats, with their long, fan-shaped tails, haunt olive groves as well as the more natural vegetation found around oases. Although normally shy birds, in the spring the males sing from prominent perches and sometimes while in flight. Fulvous babblers are present throughout the year and, although usually birds of desert areas, sometimes stray into orchards and olive groves.

PEACE AND QUIET

On the ground beneath the trees, hoopoes diligently probe with their long beaks in search of grubs, but despite their bright pink, black and white plumage, they are often inconspicuous and difficult to see.

Goats and sheep are the most numerous of man's domesticated animals in Tunisia. In many areas they graze the vegetation to such an extent that regeneration is prevented, resulting in a rather desolate appearance to the landscape. While this overgrazed environment does not favour most animals, larks and wheatears find it to their liking. The small but colourful Moussier's redstart also tolerates this type of habitat and nests in rock crevices and among boulders. Its red, black and white plumage and habit of perching conspicuously makes it easy to recognise.

Desert Life

Life for plants and animals in the desert is harsh. They have to survive not only near-drought conditions but also extremes in temperature. During the day, the blistering sun heats the surface of the soil until it can be too hot to touch, while at night the temperatures drop rapidly.

Many desert animals obtain all the moisture they need from their diet of plants or animals. Other creatures, such as sandgrouse, although supremely adapted to the rigours of desert life, are still tied to water. Flocks will fly for up to 40 miles (65km) from their breeding or feeding grounds to reach a known watering spot, generally visiting the pool at dawn or dusk. Pin-tailed sandgrouse frequent deserts and plains, especially where there are scattered tamarisk bushes to provide shade from the midday sun, while their black-bellied relatives haunt more mountainous regions. Like other species of sandgrouse, when their chicks have hatched, the parents soak their breast feathers at the drinking pools and carry this water source back to the nest scrape to quench the young's thirst. Coronated and spotted sandgrouse are also frequent in Tunisia but prefer even more desolate and arid deserts than the other species. Even where there is seemingly no vegetation at all they still manage to find the shoots and seeds which make up their diet. Coronated sandgrouse show a remarkable adaptation to dry conditions: they can even drink slightly saline water.

While on the ground, the sandy-coloured plumage of sandgrouse makes them extremely difficult to spot, and in flight, the shimmering heat haze can cause the observer problems as flocks fly fast and low to the ground. The best clues to their presence are their liquid, gurgling calls which are uttered in flight, and dawn observations in the vicinity of desert lakes are generally best. One of the major enemies of sandgrouse is the lanner falcon. This typical desert raptor often uses posts and telegraph poles

Scorpions: feared desert residents

as a lookout and with its swift and low flight it generally catches its prey in the air. Unusually for birds of prey, lanners sometimes hunt in pairs, which greatly increases their chances of success with agile quarry like sandgrouse. The intense heat of the midday desert sun is enough to cause serious problems of dehydration to most animals. Not surprisingly, many creatures avoid the excessive daytime temperatures and only move about after dark. Daylight hiding places in burrows, under boulders and in rock crevices are at a premium and few are without a resident reptile or invertebrate.

Among the most feared inhabitants of the desert are scorpions. Although they do possess a poisonous sting, the reputation of Tunisian scorpions is a little undeserved since the effects on a healthy human are seldom more than localised pain and inflammation. On a small mammal or insect, however, the effect is much more dramatic, and paralysis occurs rapidly. Thereafter, the scorpion's formidable pincers, which in many species are strong enough to crush the skull of a mouse, grip and tear the victim.

Many of the desert insects and spiders fall victim to the nocturnal stone curlew. During the daytime these secretive birds are very wary, but after dark they become active, uttering their strange and far-carrying 'curlew'-like calls. Other desert birds like the long-legged buzzard hunt by day, floating effortlessly in the

PEACE AND QUIET

rising thermals. They catch unsuspecting reptiles and birds on the ground, while Egyptian vultures prefer to scavenge the remains of the meals of others. Larks are among the best adapted and most dominant families of passerine birds in the Tunisian deserts. One of the most characteristic species is the appropriately named desert lark, although bar-tailed desert, Calandra, thick-billed, Thekla and crested larks are all widespread throughout the stony, arid plains.

Although never abundant, both hoopoe and Dupont's larks are also found in southern Tunisia. They are superficially similar, with long legs and a long, down-curved bill, but hoopoe larks are readily identified by their conspicuous black and white wings in flight. Dupont's larks, on the other hand, are rather plain and their plumage helps their excellent camouflage. Although the faint, whistling song is often heard at dawn, actually to see one of these secretive birds is a 'blue riband' day.

In the dry, open country and deserts of Tunisia, wheatears are second only to the larks in their variety and abundance. Five species are present throughout the year, their numbers being supplemented by two more species during the summer months. Other vagrant species occur during migration, making Tunisia one of the best countries in the whole of the Mediterranean region to observe these elegant, and often confiding, birds. With the exception of

red-rumped wheatear, all of Tunisia's wheatears have in common a white rump. As you drive along dusty roads or walk through scrubby habitat this conspicuous feature attracts the eye as the bird flies ahead of your progress. Wheatears are alert little birds which, because of their smart black and white plumage, are easier to spot than larks. As if to assist the birdwatcher, they often perch prominently and then their plumage can be studied in detail.

The vast, seasonally flooding salt lakes, known as *chotts*, which are found in the south of the country mark the northern limit of the Sahara. The stony arid landscape found elsewhere in Tunisia, although less dramatic, nevertheless harbours more desert wildlife. The drive from Tozeur to Kebili across Chott el Jerid can be good. Oasis towns are always especially rich. The road south from Gabes to Medenine and on to Foum Tataouine can also be good. Drive the minor roads to towns and villages off the main route.

The dry courses of seasonal rivers, know as *oueds* or *wadis*, are often favoured by wheatears, larks and sandgrouse. They provide comparatively rich feeding areas, since seeds are often carried and deposited by past rains. Occasionally, a trickle of water remains underground throughout the dry summer and this hint of moisture encourages slightly more plant and animal life than the surrounding lands.

Small flocks of barbary partridges also frequent these *oueds*, especially at higher elevations in the north of Tunisia. Barred flanks and speckled throat make this an extremely elegant bird. The male sometimes utters his loud call from rocky outcrops. Sharing the same remote and inhospitable environment are many desert mammals. Gazelles and striped hyenas are now seldom seen due to persecution. Golden jackals do occur, although their nocturnal habits mean they are more often heard than seen.

Forests

As a surprising contrast to the desert terrain and agricultural land of much of lowland Tunisia, parts of the northern mountain chain running parallel with the

Blue-cheeked bee-eaters are colourful summer visitors to Tunisia. They often perch on dead branches or overhead wires

coast have extensive forests; these comprise mainly pines and cork oaks. The woods around Aïn Draham, close to the Algerian border in north-west Tunisia are especially good. The birds and other wildlife have more in common with Europe than Africa.

Bird Migration

Tunisia and the whole of the north African coast lie at the junction of the two major hazards which face Europe's migrant birds each year: the Sahara desert and the Mediterranean sea. Over one they must fly for 1,000 miles (1,600km) without water and over the other they must cover vast expanses of sea without landfall. Not surprisingly, therefore, Tunisia is a staging post for weary birds both in spring and autumn, and oases, pools and lake margins are often thronged with migrants from March to May and from

PEACE AND QUIET

August to October.
The problem of crossing the Sahara is, for many species, getting worse because in effect the desert is gradually extending further and further south. The traditional wintering grounds for many species of birds was the Sahel region to the south of the desert proper. These areas of seasonal and unpredictable rain had, for centuries, been lush in winter, providing rich feeding grounds for the migrants. For several years, however, the rains in the Sahel were either poor or failed completely and the land became parched and barren. The drought led not only to human misery, but also to the birds losing their winter refuges. Consequently, each year they had to fly further and further south to find food, and many did not survive the journey. Swallows and martins suffered greatly from this disappearance of wintering grounds and numbers of sand martins in particular dropped to an all-time low in their northern European breeding grounds. However, recent rains may lead to an increase in numbers, and despite the difficulties faced by the birds south of the Sahara, hundreds of thousands still pass through Tunisia each spring. Noisy parties of bee-eaters are a frequent sight around oases and on telegraph wires beside roads. Blue-cheeked bee-eaters, resplendent with their almost metallic green plumage, are welcome visitors to dry, stony plains and hills and are sometimes seen perched on bushes along dry riverbeds.

Although they are not thought to breed in Tunisia, small parties are common in spring, and during the summer they often stray into Tunisia from their breeding grounds in Algeria.

The Ship of the Desert
The domesticated camel is a remarkable animal that is superbly adapted to life in the deserts, which it once roamed wild. Its relationship with man has lasted for centuries and it is a crucial factor in the lives of nomadic peoples of North Africa and the Middle East. The Camel has a lifespan of 25 years, enough time for its master to get to know its foibles. Dromedary camels, with their single hump, are used as beasts of burden, but are also important for their milk, meat and wool and are sometimes even raced.
Although seemingly docile most of the time, they are frequently stubborn and bad-tempered and often try to bite their owners.
Camels are renowned for their ability to survive long periods without water. If not working, they have been known to go for 10 months without a drink, the water requirements of their bodies being met by their famous humps, which are storage places for fat. The plants they eat also provide moisture. They conserve what water they have extremely well and produce almost dry faeces and very little urine.
After a long period of enforced dehydration, camels quench their thirst by drinking vast quantities of water, 28 gallons (130 litres) or more not being unusual in a single session.

FOOD AND DRINK

Food

Tunisia has a wide selection of speciality dishes. Europeans usually find those served in most homes so highly spiced that they can scarcely distinguish one dish from the next. In most hotels, on the other hand, the dishes are made so tame for visitors that, again, one scarcely tastes different from the next. The best European cuisine can be had in the better restaurants of Tunis, Hammamet or Sousse. The beach hotels offer the occasionally successful 'native

dish', but it is the local 'Arab' restaurants that should be recommended for *spécialités tunisiennes*. In every town there are several where you can eat with impunity; the waiters will be willing and the décor simple or traditional. These notes may help with menus:

Brik – a semi circle of super-light pastry (called *malsuka*) filled with either egg, spinach or a meat/tunnyfish mix and deep-fried. It is cheap and delicious. You should, like the Tunisians, eat it with your fingers: take a corner in each hand and bite boldly into the stuffed part.

Chakchouka – Tunisians speak proudly of this national dish of tomatoes, pimentoes and garlic with a poached egg on top –

Fish and vegetable couscous: the semolina grain made from remoistened hard wheat has become Tunisia's culinary symbol

FOOD AND DRINK

and very tasty it is.

Chorba tunisienne – Tunisian soup. Chefs pass it off as a speciality: in fact it is an umbrella-term under which they can serve tomato soup, vegetable soup, fish soup etc which would be sent back if the menu said Tomato Soup, Vegetable Soup, Fish Soup etc. However, *if* prepared properly, spiced and sprinkled with lemon juice, *chorba hout* (Tunisian fish soup) can be delectable. *Leblabi* you see less often and *mdames* less still. They are both broths, consisting of chick-peas and green beans respectively, with *harissa* (red pepper sauce) and spices to taste.

Couscous – a national symbol. (Tunisian blurb-writers talk of their 'Land of the Couscous'.) It is a semolina grain made, like spaghetti and macaroni, from hard wheat. Housewives remoisten the dried grains and cook a kneaded mass of them in a special colander, the *couscoussier*, in the steam of the boiling fish, meat or vegetables. The result should be pleasantly light, with a mild savour of the particular fish, meat or vegetable. Slightly livelier is sweet couscous (*mesfuf*) mixed with nuts and raisins.

Fish come singly, fried as entrées, or in *complets de poisson* complete with fried egg, chips, tomatoes, maybe peas and certainly pimentoes. Tunisia's fish are not only food but good-luck charms as well: they are painted on the walls of houses or sculpted in door-surrounds, they are

Brik à l'oeuf: the light, fan-shaped pastry can also be filled with spinach or a meat/tunnyfish mix

presented to newly-wed couples and worn by women round their necks or on their clothes in paper, cloth or plastic cut-outs. Few appreciate that the emblem derives from the classical, fertility-bringing, stylised phallus.

Kaftaji (*dyari*) – basically seasoned meat-balls, fried and served with cubes of liver, peppers, onions and courgettes.

Kamounia – a savoury and filling plateful of cubed liver and stewed meat in thick gravy, taking its name and flavour from the cumin seed.

Koucha – mutton, ideally shoulder of lamb, roasted whole with chillies and potatoes.

Mechoui – the French form of the Arabic for 'roasted', used in Tunisia for roast lamb.

Mechouia, on the other hand, is a salad – a cubed and diced mixture, not as light as you might expect, of charcoal-grilled peppers, tomatoes and onions or garlic, doused in lemon juice, vinegar and oil, and decorated with capers, parsley and hard-boiled egg.

Merguez – a hard and highly spiced sausage.

Mirmiz – stewed mutton, simmered with broad beans and served together with a piquant sauce.

Ojja – preferable with brains but possible with *merguez*: a panful of scrambled egg and red peppers simmered in butter and olive oil, with tomato purée and/or *harissa* (red pepper sauce), and the meat added afterwards. In local restaurants an overdose of *harissa* often overpowers everything.

Shellfish are a delicacy abundant in Tunisian waters, but lobsters (*homards*), oysters (*huîtres*), clams (*clovisses*), mussels (*moules*), shrimps (*crevettes*) and king prawns (*crevettes royales*) do not differ from the best in Europe.

Tajine or *tajine malsuka* – a tasty left-overs dish, that is served hot or cold, in heavy squares like yellowing bread pudding or larger and round, and with the chunks of meat set in a solid centre of egg and cheese. Probably none the less tasty for the meat being yesterday's left-overs.

Drink

Time was – just after World War II – when French bottlers sold cheap Algerian Wine in Europe as *Vin de Tunisie*. (They did Tunisia an inverse injustice with her first-class *Deglat Nur* dates.) For a Muslim country (Islam disapproves of alcohol), Tunisia nowadays produces some very fine wines.

The best are now trickling, despite the 'wine lake', on to the European market (which may explain their unpredictable availability here): *Sidi Saad*, a heavy red, distinctively bottled in green-glass amphorae, twin-handled and labelled in

FOOD AND DRINK

German; the suaver red *La Bonne Bouteille* and *Château Feriani*; *Clairet de Bizerte* and, since 1980, the rosé *Gris de Tunisie*, which is close to but not quite a *Coteaux d'Aix*. You find *Coteaux de Carthage* and *de Tebourba* in red, white and rosé, *d'Utique* in red only and *de Hammamet* in red or rosé. Also very palatable are red *Lamblot* and *Château Mornag*, and red or rosé *Thyna* and *Magon*. *Dougga* is a dependable *rosé muscaté* and, available as white or rosé, *Sidi Rais* has a very marked bouquet. Hotels in which the Carte des Vins is sparse usually plump for the trusty *Tardi*, *Thibar* and *Haut Mornag*, *Hidalgo*, *Domaine Karim*, *Carthage* and *Koudiat*, most of which come in red, rosé or white. The cheaper, coarser *Sidi Naceur*, *Rossel*, *Grombalia* and *Zarrour* remain village tipplers' favourites. Discerning drinkers prefer them mixed with water or clear lemonade, a mixture which Tunisians call 'Maltese champagne'.

All wines are medium dry except for the muscats (exception made of the *Muscat sec de Kelibia*). The muscats have body enough to make an enjoyable aperitif. Being fairly inexpensive in the shops, a bottle of Tunisian wine is worth taking home (and should travel well). When they see the price of imported champagne, jet-setters settle for the local *Médaillon Vert*. It is reasonably cheap, and sweet, but tastes as though it has already travelled badly before you buy it.

Except aboard Tunis Air, half or smaller bottles are rare; if you are dining alone and/or feel daunted by a full bottle, most *maître d'*'s will set aside the rest for your next meal. While wine is very varied, beer is almost monopolistically *Celtia* – brewed in Tunis, sold in bottles or (on Tunis Air) in cans, and somewhere between lager and light ale. In 1984 *Celtia Extra Dry 33* was launched, in lieu of the short-lived Tunis-made *Tuborg*. Only *Stella* is a malty alternative, marketed in bigger bottles which few hotels stock.

For shandy (or Maltese champagne) all these can be mixed with clear *Boga* lemonade. Coca-, Pepsi- or 'Royal Crown' Cola is the usual palliative for Tunisia's pet spirit *Boukha*. This fire-water is distilled from figs, most popular as an aperitif and easily, when ordered, confused with *Boga...* and with noxious results. A surprisingly smooth Tunisian liqueur is *Thibarine*.

Boga on one of the bar's stock of *sirops* – green *menthe*, red *grenadine*, white *orgeat* – makes a refreshing and eye-catching cordial.

Given the reservations over tap-water, you might well prefer the several cheap and excellent, bottled, natural and/or mineral equivalents: *Aïn Garci*, quite pleasantly aerated (and no bad soda-substitute in whisky);. *Aïn Oktor*, flat and slightly soapy; *Safia*, *Melliti* and the newer *Koutine*, flat and similar to *Vichy*. The national drink, mint tea, is served in tiny glasses.

The distinctive bright colours and striking designs of Tunisia's rugs, klims and runners

SHOPPING

Tunisia has an excellent selection of local crafts. In every main town there are branches of the governmental National Handicrafts Office (*ONA*, or ask for *l'Artisanat*), and the Tunis headquarters (on the corner of the Avenues de Carthage and Bourguiba, and also on the Avenue Mohammed V) are very well-stocked museums of fashion and furnishings, with the exhibits on sale at fixed prices. Most hotels have their

boutiques and bazaars or pseudo-suqs (Arab markets). Contents vary slightly, and again the price is fixed. It will generally be lower than what local shops and suqs ask at first but not as low as the figure you can often beat them down to. 'This carpet, Madam, is 500 years old. But for you we'll make it 300.' The funnier suq-salesmen's patter sets the tone for their give-and-take attitude to bartering. So do not be bashful. If the shopkeeper opens with prices optimistic if not downright preposterous, do not dismiss them indignantly but take them as an 'invitation to treat'. A third or so of the price first asked is

SHOPPING

your best opening offer: make it less and you may be snubbed. If trade is bad and no other buyers are in sight, you should settle at around half-price without too much ado. If not, just pretend to leave: that should change the salesman's tune. Time spent inspecting several shops will show vendors that you are serious and they should then make their prices more attractive. There may also be others in the hotel with similar purchases in mind – if you unite, prices fall.

Boutiques and ONA (National Handicraft Office) shops sell updated Tunisian clothes

The best buys in Tunisia are leather-, metal- and woodwork, ceramics and pottery, local clothes and carpets. The last take pride of place. Though modern products are chiefly of the type that the Turks brought in from Persia, carpet-making here is a time-honoured craft. When homes were goat's-hair tents, the carpet was the household's focal centre (like the open fireplace in pre-war homes – or the TV today). The beduin family's herds of sheep and goats provided the raw material, and the womenfolk the work. This began in spring when the sheep were sheared; the rising heat of summer then dried the washed, spun wool, that was dyed with herbs, roots and fruit.

Natural dye-stuff went out with World War II, and home wool supplies could not long keep pace with the thriving industry that weaving soon became. Beside the ubiquitous workshops, every large bazaar from Bizerta to Tozeur has girls on low benches at tall looms working (and chattering) for eight hours per day. They use 'knotted point', with 10,000–490,000 points to the square metre. Only on Jerba are carpets and tugs made, mostly by men, in 'short nap'. On-the-spot weaving in the resorts naturally invalidates traditional designations of origin and style. At its Den-Den workshops near Tunis, for example, the ONA manufactures a fine range of 'Kairouan' carpets. This type also comes to Sousse and Hammamet from the Sahel villages of Khnis, Ksibet and Lamta, Moknine, Sayada and Ksar Hellal. Most popular is the *zerbia* with its discreet geometry and subdued natural hues evolved in Kairouan in the 1830s. The *mergum*, too, originated there, when the Zarrouk family thought of copying on carpets the patterns embroidered on the Berber women's bodices.

Ceramics, clothes and the ubiquitous carpets are tempting items but be ready to haggle

More regionally authentic (but also on sale everywhere), the tugs and covers of Gafsa and Gabes are unmistakable in their nursery colours and Paul Klee motifs. All are called loosely *klim* or *hanbal*, though the latter is strictly a blanket, a Berber wedding-present in natural-coloured wool, and the *klim* traditionally anything red. Oudref was famous for its *bishts* (saddle-covers) and still has a couple of *bisht*-makers left.

Both designs and prices are tempting. Tunisian carpets are none the less valuables and, unless you have come prepared, you will need the COD system (10 per cent down) that most sellers offer. It is reliable. And the British

SHOPPING

An attractive and fragrant array: perfumes in a Tunis shop

Customs now demand only 17½ per cent for VAT (the Americans nil), providing you can prove that your import comes from Tunisia. Sheepskins and rush mats make a rather cheaper covering for your floor. The latter orginate in scattered, unexpected marshes such as Somaa's. The cut rushes come down, most in June and July, to Nabeul and Houmt Souk, where you can watch the boys weaving cross-legged at their horizontal looms. The end product, attractive in gold with motifs in black, is sold either by the metre for floor covering, runners and table-mats, or shaped into lampshades, wastepaper-baskets, poufs and popular, black-handled bags decorated with a camel, 'Nabeul' or your name. The matting is not as cheap as it looks but the poufs are a hard-wearing bargain. Sheepskins have been the obvious victim of increased demand for carpet-wool and a new concern for leather, and Tunisia's leather-workers have reacted predictably to soaring prices in Europe. The old lines have been maintained: wallets, caskets, handbags, book covers, desk equipment and *babouches* (pointed slippers), all functional in natural shades, or dyed red or green and gold-incised. Leather poufs have always been popular. On those under 10 dinars make sure the seams are strong; more elaborate patterns, sometimes worked in gold, will make the price higher. Pinned nowadays above every other work-bench, cuttings from Italian catalogues reveal the latest source of inspiration. This new Tunisian *maroquinerie* makes for stylish bargains, if not 'local colour': tanned professionally supple and strongly sewn, dyed and modelled to match the fashionable foreign lines which it undercuts.

The uprooting, for the sake of 'development', of olive-groves everywhere has given a fillip to woodcarving. Old hat are the olive-wood boxes, bowls and utensils, plus the same gazelles and sucking fawns as appear, mutated into antelopes, identically stylised in East and West Africa. In natural finish or high gloss, this traditional range has been enlarged to anything workable in wood, from combs to hat-stands.

In many resorts young craftsmen incise minor masterpieces in brass and will inscribe them to order (but do watch their spelling). Tunisian birdcages are catching on even in European capitals at inflated prices. These blue-and-white delights of ornate wire and wood, varying with size and quality from 4 to 12

A craftsman at work on his brass and copperware stall in Nabeul

dinars, are now made as often in Raf-Raf as in their namesake Sidi Bou Said.

The widest and cheapest range of Tunisian specialities is undoubtedly in earthenware: glazed plates inscribed in Arabic (or with camels and palms); beakers, lampshades and plain ingenious ash-trays; monstrous urns and tall, shapely pitchers; elegant dinner-services, gross glossy ducks and cocks which are tureens or table centre-pieces, dinky musicians ruddy-buff in terracotta. Nabeul makes most, but from Guellala on Jerba come some pretty curiosities:

SHOPPING

pots with rims irregularly 'crenellated' so that fitting the lid is a puzzle, and jugs which you fill from the top, then the bottom, without a drop leaking either way. The potters work in three grades of clay: cheap reddish buff, better creamy white and fine grey kaolin. On the glazed ware, patterns are traditionally flowery or birdy and the colours green, yellow and manganese-brown, though Nabeul's potters are now turning their hand to anything that sells.

Traditional dress designs have been adapted and updated, best by the various ONA stores and the Boutique Fella in Hammamet. In Mahdia gold-sequinned wedding-jackets are still embroidered by the womenfolk at home, and hawked at the Friday morning market. Nabeul's market sells the heavy perfumes from local flowers for which that town is known. Embroidery is an old-established craft best observed in the museums' displays of traditional dress. To complete your Tunisian ensemble there are some good-value silver rings – *métal argenté*, worked usually in the lucky Fatma's Hand or fish emblems – and either chunky beduin bangles or necklaces and pendants in delicate filigree work. (One specialist is the Bazar de la Kasbah, its whereabouts obvious in Hammamet.) Tunisian gold and silver you buy for the workmanship, not as a metal investment.

On every ancient site you will be offered Roman and Byzantine coins, openly by the locals and surreptitiously by the official *gardien*. Should any be authentic, the price will be high. Most will be cheap because labour is too – present-day labour, in the back-room 'mints' of Tunis. Apart from the occasional coin, do not expect antiques. The carpets have all been donated to the mosques and only in Tunis, with much perseverance, will you find any interesting *objets d'art*. Ayoub's, on the Avenue Habib Bourguiba and in the medina, are expensive and mostly imported pastiche; Evangelisti's, also in the Rue Jamaa ez-Zitouna and the Hammamet medina, are more varied, authentic and typically Tunisian. Two 'antique' lines have been actively revived: old-fashioned soldier-dolls (arthritic marionettes) and industrial samples of the now vanishing handicraft of 'reversal' painting on glass (usually only of crude, scimitar-wielding warriors). With its heavy import duty, Tunisia is no Mediterranean Hong Kong for cheap watches and cameras. Customs officials know this and tend to be lenient with returning holidaymakers. (The USA aids Tunisia's economy by admitting most items duty free.) Besides the drink and cigarettes from the Tunisian duty free shops or the stewardess, you are entitled to export £32/$400 worth of presents. (The Customs are a lot wiser than you think to 'cut-price' receipts.)

Tunisian-style refreshments at a Hammamet hotel

ACCOMMODATION

Tunisia woke up to tourism in the 1960s and very few resort hotels are not modern and well designed. The *Société Hôtelière et Touristique de Tunisie* had been established with government backing in 1959 to pioneer hotel-building: its rapid success allayed the fears of private investors and now Tunisia possesses over 200 first-class hotels. Almost all are privately owned and managed, usually by international chains, by a handful of Tunisian tycoons or by syndicates of local businessmen backed by State or foreign investment.

In 1974–5 the *Office National du Tourisme Tunisien* (*ONTT*) introduced a much-needed classification programme allotting one to four stars, or 'four stars *luxe*' to the very best hotels. This classification is, on the whole, good, and the stars awarded are given in the text. However, the authorities took into account only physical criteria such as room dimensions and equipment and numbers of personnel: they did not, understandably, attempt to assess human factors like technical competence, politeness and general amiability. Be sure to bear in mind, therefore, that a hotel in which the staff are friendly and efficient and the manager affable may have fewer stars than another which has unskilled employees and an arrogant or wholly inaccessible manager, but with marginally larger rooms and an extra bedside table.

NIGHTLIFE AND ENTERTAINMENT

Almost all resort hotels have disco, or dancing to live music in the bar, and there are independent nightclubs or discos in every resort except Tabarka. With tasteful lighting and décor, the right climate for romantic patios and generally excellent Tunisian or Italian bands playing European music, they are all that most people want after a long and enjoyable day in the sun.

Floorshows are limited to *le folklore* – dancing girls gorgeously (and fully) clad in traditional silks and bangles, who move arms, hips and ankles in particular to the wail and beat of a *zukra* and *tabel* (pipe and drum). The girls often insist on audience participation,

and sometimes the musicians play and gyrate with rather more suggestiveness than grace. It is the sort of show you could watch for hours if only they would turn down the sound. Half an hour of this is nearer the norm for the package party's standard evening out: coach-ride to one of the custom-built nightspots, canteen dinner while the local star dances, wine galore to help you bear the music, and perhaps a juggler, performing with pots, or maybe even a snake-charmer stealing the show by draping snakes round ladies' necks.

Real belly-dancing is rare: only at certain restaurants in Tunis can you regularly see

'Folklore' floorshows are a frequent feature of the tourist package

dancing girls, usually Egyptian, with sufficient mammary dexterity to give a show that is exotic and not vulgar.

Hoteliers periodically change the attractions from nightly dancing by arranging film or conjuring shows and barbecues on the beach or by the pool.

By day, the beach will monopolise most of your time. Here the unlikely star-cum-curiosity is the camel: either the one-humped Arabian, or dromedary. Hotels rarely deign to own one but allow local cameleers to give rides on the beach or up the *oued*. 'Ride' is a relative term: except on the 'Mini-Safari' excursions, which include real camel treks over the Sahara, your beach parade on a camel's back is not so much like riding as a session in the gym. Be prepared for the sharp, steep, three-stage rise. Tunisia's horses are either Arab, with a straight nose, a high tail and an impressive turn of speed, or Berber, convex-nosed and bred for sturdy work. In either case do not expect any very expert dressage: they need mastering from the word go, and can jerk from a listless amble to a fearsome gallop at the slightest provocation. Many hotels give rides, but not lessons. If your interest in horses is more sedate, you can watch Arab and English thoroughbreds race most Sunday afternoons from October to June at Ksar Said, an easy taxi-ride from Tunis.

While the rockier coasts round Tabarka, Bizerta, northern Cap Bon, Monastir and Mahdia are splendid for skin-diving and snorkelling, the shore at Hammamet, Sousse and Jerba is more for sailing and windsurfing. With gentle breezes all the year round, dinghy sailors are invariably delighted. Off Hammamet and Monastir, however, the winds and currents are such that hotels will not often allow them to take out a hotel boat alone. Skimming full-sailed (or pushing their boards swimming), windsurfers now outnumber sailors off every summer beach. There is often on-shore instruction, with learners on boardless sails falling about in the sand. Those hotels with the likes of mini-golf do not mind their being used – and paid for – by residents of neighbouring establishments. The same thing applies to tennis-courts, the country's hotels now being so well-equipped as to warrant a special leaflet *Tennis in Tunisia* (available from the Tourist Offices, see page 123). With 30 floodlit courts and a 'Masters Restaurant', the leitmotif of Gammarth's Cap Carthage Hotel needs no explaining. Likewise the 'Hôtel Tennis Méditerranée/Open Club' at El Kantaoui, while in most coast hotels four or five courts is average and up to a dozen not exceptional.

Golf has also come into its own. Tunisia teed off with the 18-hole tournament course landscaped by Californians at El Kantaoui – over 254 acres (103ha) of olive-slopes beside the sea. In 1988 Ronald Fream completed another 18-hole, par 72 course of 6,700 yards (6,125m) near by at Monastir, and there is a third 18-hole, par 72 course alongside the motorway into Hammamet.

WEATHER AND WHEN TO GO

From Cap Bon in northern Tunisia you can, on a clear day, see Sicily; the country's southern half extends deep into the desert. The climate of the well-watered north is thus predictably Mediterranean and that of the far south, Saharan. Coastal resorts both north and south are, however, tempered by perennial sea-breezes that make the summer sun enjoyable and the winter weather generally fine for every outdoor activity except swimming (unless your hotel boasts a heated pool). The summer breezes can be deceptive. Even if the air feels

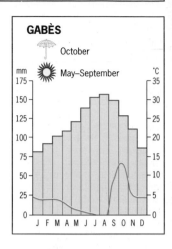

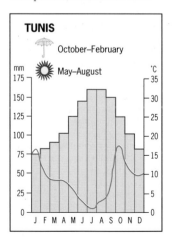

cool, remember the sun is African. Bazaars and local shops sell various sun creams (though the prices make it worth while arriving well supplied). Summer temperatures can rise in places to over 100°F (38°C) and sticklers for statistics may feel a need for the following official reassurance: that the August average for the last 50 years is 86°F (30°C) in Sousse, 84°F (29°C) in Tabarka, 86°F (30°C) in Hammamet, 86°F (30°C) on Jerba and a mere 90°F (32°C) in Tozeur, the most Saharan of Tunisian towns.

Everywhere, May and June are the most enjoyable months: flowers bloom the year round but at that time the colours and abundance are delightful. July and August are best for serious sun-tanning, although half-days of rain come regularly as a persistent surprise. In autumn the air and the sea are as limpid and warm as in spring; only the greenery has dulled in the summer sun. November rains can vary from momentary showers to cloudbursts. And in 'winter', which can start as early as October or as late as December and can give way to hot, dry weather any time between February and April, you can shiver in bright sunshine or be warm in a thunderstorm. Frosts are rare, mists rarer.

When to go and what to wear depends on all the above. Even in the heat of July and August air-conditioned coaches can still make visits to the Tunisian Sahara pleasant (but do wear 100 per cent cotton rather than synthetic fibre).

Muslims preparing for prayer

HOW TO BE A LOCAL

It would obviously be inappropriate to offer non-Arab holiday-makers advice on 'being a local' in an Arab land. Awareness of local sensitivities is another matter.

Despite the fact that Tunisia is the most liberal of Arab nations, visitors should be prepared for a difference in attitudes and expectations. These differences may be brought home particularly to lone female travellers, despite the fact that Tunisian women now enjoy an increasing degree of liberty. But good sense and respect for custom and tradition will solve most difficulties (see **Directory, Personal Safety**, page 119). On the whole, friendliness and hospitality are the hallmarks of Tunisians, and goodwill and courtesy from their visitors never go amiss.

SPECIAL EVENTS

There are many and various local events: the following is only a limited selection. See also respective individual cities and sites.

April: Ulysses Festival, Jerba.
June: Sparrow-Hawk Festival, El Haouraria; drama performances, Dougga Roman theatre.
July/August: Carthage Festival; Hammamet Festival; Monastir Festival; Festival of Aoussou, Sousse; Tabarka Festival.
November/December: Tozeur Festival; Carthage Film Festival (biennial); Sahara Festival, Douz.

CHILDREN

Tunisians make no apparent effort to cater specifically for youngsters. They don't need to. Children – boys in particular – enjoy a special place in their society and the interest and care shown for visitors' children is rarely any less. Allowing only for height-of-summer sun and the hazards of traffic, you can without a qualm let toddlers romp or teenagers explore without risk of child molesting of any kind. Beaches in all the resorts slope gently and are safe; most hotels have children's pools; camel- and horse-riding is safer with sand to fall off in, and the only potential (and ironical) hazards are the children's playgrounds in some hotel gardens, which are badly maintained or even rusting and broken.

Tunis Air offers 50 per cent off full fare for up to 12-year-olds on some flights, and most tour operators give substantial (and variable) children's reductions. Certain hotels advertise evening babysitters, but do check on availability (and reliability).

On the other hand, some tour operators have qualified 'children's representatives' to organise games and entertainment, supervise early suppers and mind infants until parents return.

TIGHT BUDGET

Tunisian workers live and raise (often very large) families on only 5 dinars per day and, if prepared to 'go native', you need spend little more than this.

Some tips which you may find useful include:

● The fare is the first hurdle: last-minute sales of seats on charter flights can be surprisingly low. Or hitch-hike to Sicily and sail deck-class by Tirrenia ferry from Trapani to Tunis/La Goulette.

● The immigration police at ports and airports do not encourage footloose travellers and require the name of your hotel on the immigration form – so have a name, any name, ready.

● Hitch-hiking is common amongst the locals (who may have to pay towards the petrol) and not over-exploited by tourists. Few Tunisian drivers, especially in remote areas, would in fact refuse a lift to clean and honest-looking Europeans. (But the unkempt or excessively hirsute may even be refused service in banks and 'better' places.) Otherwise, travel by train on the main north-south line, by *louage*-taxi if you dare, or (best) by local bus.

● Eat at the *gargotes* the locals (men only) use, or buy bread and fresh fruit from the local market.

● Take with you some kind of upset-stomach tablets for when drivers give you not only lifts but meals too, and a cotton sleeping bag for when a bed is offered.

● There are youth hostels at Nabeul (behind the esplanade), Tunis Medina, Kelêbia and at Zarzis and Gabes (found near the ONA).

DIRECTORY

Arriving

● **By Air** Tunis Air, the country's national airline, has one of the world's best safety records. Tunis Air's pilots show up European colleagues with the sheer smoothness of their take-offs and landings; its meals rarely fail to disappoint.

To protect Tunis Air and sell more scheduled seats, the Tunisian authorities tried for years to stop European operators offering 'flight only' fares on charter aircraft. Having failed to beat them, Tunis Air has joined them: an economy seat on its scheduled services costs full fare if bought direct, or approximately half via a tour operator.

● **By Sea** Excellent ferries from the Continent make driving well worth considering. From the Ponte Colombo in Genoa the *Habib* sets sail weekly for the 24-hour crossing. The *Habib* is the flagship of the *Compagnie Tunisienne de Navigation* – and a foretaste of Tunisia from the moment you embark. An alternative port of embarkation is Marseilles, whence the 463 sea-miles (857km) to Tunis/La Goulette are comfortably covered in 24 hours by the ferries *Habib* and *Liberté*. The *Liberté* ups anchor for Tunis from La Joliette weekly in winter, more frequently in summer. A shorter, 8-hour route is from Trapani in Sicily. On arrival with a vehicle, produce a full driving licence, log book and green-card insurance covering Tunisia, the details are entered in your passport and you may then drive for up to three months. This may on expiry be extended in Tunis by paying road and tyre tax at the central Customs – a costly operation in money, time and patience. A stay of over six months entails a residence permit, import licence and payment of duty at amazing rates.

● **Passports and Visas** A full British Citizen's or one-year British Visitor's passport entitles you to a three-month stay without a visa, as does a Canadian passport. A US passport entitles you to four months' stay. Australian and Commonwealth citizens and other UK categories should

Sunset over Skanes

check with the consular section of the Tunisian Embassy (29 Prince's Gate, London SW7 1QG, tel: 0171-584 8117).

Camping

Though the Ministry of Youth and Sports runs official campsites for Scouts and school parties, Tunisia has very few organised public facilities (on the beach near Bizerta, at Remel Plage; at Nabeul's Les Jasmins and Hammamet's 'Idéal Camping'; the Sidi Ali Club at Jerba's Sidi Slim Hotel and in the oasis of Tozeur).

Except on tourist beaches, however, you are free to pitch tents anywhere scenic and suitable (having asked the landowner's permission – if you can locate him). The local police may well stop by to check your passport, share a cigarette and (if too close to frontiers, barracks etc.) show you an alternative site.

Most petrol stations have taps for drinking-water and sell fuel for primus stoves; but camping gas is a problem, being unavailable in portable bottles and banned on your flight out.

Chemists see Pharmacies

Customs Regulations

At Tunisia's international airports and the ferry terminal at La Goulette, the Customs are categorical. A person aged 18 or over may import the following free of duty: 1 litre of spirits, 2 litres of wine; 400 cigarettes or 100 cigars or 500 grammes of tobacco; 2 cameras, 1 ciné/video camera, 20 rolls

film; 1 litre toilet water; ¼ litre perfume; gifts to the value of 10 Tunisian dinar; 1 portable radio, 1 tape recorder, 1 record player, 1 musical instrument; 2 perambulators, 1 bicycle, 1 typewriter; 1 set camping equipment, binoculars, sports gear.

The regulations, though, are relaxed for holiday-makers, and the officials' occasionally fierce approach is rarely followed by confiscation or an actual demand for payment for excess tobacco or drinks. Only obvious valuables may be noted in your passport, to be produced and checked out when you leave.

Disabled Visitors

For the less active or physically handicapped arriving by ferry, the *Liberté* sails from Marseilles to Tunis with *cabines pour handicapés*. On arrival by air, ground staff are always helpful. The Tunisian organisation *Association Generale des Insuffisants Moteurs de Tunis* may be able to deal with specific queries from disabled visitors on the spot. Before a trip, the Holiday Care Service (2, Old Bank Chambers, Horley, Surrey, tel: 01293 774535) can supply travellers with their fact sheet on Tunisian hotels offering facilities for the disabled.

Driving

On the road, your licence, passport and rental agreement (or log book and insurance – see **Arriving**, **By Sea**, page 113) have all to be produced to the police patrolmen who may stop you for a check and a chat. Should any document have been forgotten, your passport or driving licence will be taken to the local police station and released on production of the missing document.

Watch out when driving, for unlit camel-carts, donkeys and locals: if roads were meant for motors and pavements for pedestrians, Tunisia must have the finest pavement-network in the world.

Roads generally are good. Save on the main exits from Tunis and Sousse and the motorway south to Hammamet, the carriageway is narrow; but a car-wide shoulder between the road and the ritual ditch and eucalyptus adds to the width. Some roads in the south are unsurfaced, check conditions before setting out (car hire firms ban the use of their vehicles on such roads). Road signs and regulations conform to the French system; you drive on the right and signposts, in French and/or Arabic are sensibly positioned. (Even each scarcely perceptible *oued* is named). Excellent everywhere (when not defaced) are the *bornes kilométriques* (metric milestones) that line every highway, each with its number and the distance to the next centre. On the open road there is a theoretical speed limit of 55 miles (90km) per hour or 68 miles (110km) on the only motorway. This drops down in built-up areas to 31 miles (50km) per hour and, as they may fine offenders on the spot, the police are keen.

● **Car Breakdown**

The Touring Club de Tunisia provides breakdown assistance but there are no emergency

Tourist development has been rapid since the 1960s, and most resort hotels are modern and comfortable

roadside telephones. In case of breakdown, either wait (on motorway and main roads) for the fairly frequent patrol cars of the *Garde Nationale*, or wave down the next vehicle for a lift to the nearest village to find the police and/or a *mécanicien*. With a hired car, or by night, you can look to the police to contact the hirer for a replacement, or to arrange accommodation. Otherwise, the state of many cars on the road is a tribute to the Tunisians' ability to keep wrecks running: your breakdown would have to be catastrophic for the local workshop not to be able to fix it

DIRECTORY

(temporarily at least). Labour is cheap, spare parts are expensive (and have often to be fetched from main dealers in Tunis, Sousse or Sfax). Loyalty to 'approved dealerships' and 'genuine spare parts' is misplaced here: it is better to bear with the village fixer than insist on being towed to main dealers, who are over-priced, over-worked and unimpressed by emergencies.

● **Car Hire**

At the international airports and in every resort are branches of Tunisia's main hirers: Hertz, Avis, Europcar, Africar, Budget, National, InterRent and Azur. Their prices – for the usual daily/weekly plus kilometre rates – are increased by various taxes, and end up such that a 10–15 per cent discount can often be held out for on any plausible pretext. Combined with the high price of petrol, the final cost of a hired car here is greater than anywhere in Europe, and is therefore best shared by three or four. Drivers should also bear in mind – and passengers be warned – that, until it stopped disclosing such unflattering facts, Tunisia occupied second place in UN statistics for accidents per vehicle/mile. Affluence has meant that there are now far more cars than competent drivers.

Hirers require both a hefty deposit and a full licence held for over one year by drivers over 21.

● **Chauffeur Driven Cars**

If you haven't your licence, or the nerve to drive, take one of the chauffeurs that the better car-hire companies offer. Given the high cost of hiring, and low local wages, the extra expense is very relative. Your chauffeur should know enough English to be an adequate guide.

● **Driving in the Desert**

Driving in the desert is dangerous – many inexperienced travellers die there each year. For your own protection, tell the *Garde Nationale* where you plan to go and check in with them on arrival. Ensure your vehicle is suitable for off-road driving, travel with at least one other vehicle, check your fuel (carry some spare), oil and water; take tools, spare tyres, a shovel and

A Tunisian with the hump: one of the 'ships of the desert'

matting. Carry water, blankets and suncreams for passengers. In the event of a breakdown, stay with the vehicle, to avoid dying from the heat (around 104°F/40°C) or getting lost.

Electricity

The current in Tunisia is 220 volts, except in those parts of Tunis where 110 voltage is common. Sockets are of the two round-pin variety.

Embassies and Consulates

Canada: 3 Rue Didon, Tunis (tel: 01 286 577). (Also handles Australian affairs.)
UK: 5 Place de la Victoire, Tunis (tel: 01 245 100); (consulate) 141–3 Avenue de la Liberté (tel: 01 287 293)
USA: 144 Avenue de la Liberté, Tunis (tel: 01 282 566)

Emergency Telephone Numbers

National emergency number: 197
Ambulance: 491 313
Doctors: contact hotel desk
Police: 197
Fire: 198

Health Requirements

Always check with your doctor on the current health situation about a month before your planned holiday (outbreaks of disease can occur). Check up on your immunisation against Hepatitis A, typhoid and polio, and tetanus protection. You may want a cholera injection and/or a course of malaria pills. Tunisian water is not the tapped miasma that you should avoid at all costs. Locals and expatriates drink it and thrive. Only

sometimes in summer do the authorities overreact to any possible risk: they chlorinate unpleasantly, almost opaquely. Although quite safe to clean teeth in, the water at any time of year is sufficiently different to combine, occasionally, with the change of food and climate and perturb stomachs. 'The trots', 'Gippy tummy' here becomes 'Hannibal's revenge' – an open-ended, half-day upset and the only health hazard to which Westerners seem prone. (By pouring iced drinks into sunbathing bodies you can make it self-inflicted.) Only hotels inland and in the oases might be thought to need summer air-conditioning. Few others have indulged in this pointless expense and there is thus little risk of colds and bronchial problems when coming in from the heat to icy air-conditioned rooms.
Most hotels have a house doctor on (usually prompt) call. In the absence of a national health service, doctors and pharmacists are prosperous and numerous. It is a crass, sweeping and valid generalisation that, unlike the local hospitals, most are good. You pay on the spot for any treatment so health insurance is advisable. Europ Assistance (252 High Street, Croydon CR0 1NF, tel: 0181-680 1234) will, for a surprisingly cheap premium, lay on a prompt and private jet for emergency flights home. A mile from Monastir airport, the Chems Hotel (tel: 03 66 288) has a professionally run sick-bay for temporary treatment whilst awaiting transportation.

DIRECTORY

Ojja – a meal in a pan: scrambled egg, red peppers and merguez

Holidays

The Islamic equivalents of Christmas, New Year and Easter (and which everyone observes) are *Mouled* (the Prophet Mohammed's supposed birthday), *Ras El Am El Hejri* (New Year's Day), the '*Id el Fitr* (or '*Id es-Saghir*, the 'Small Feast' that ends the month-long fast of Ramadhan) and the '*Id el Adha* (or '*Id el Kebir*, the 'Great Feast'). All follow the Islamic calendar. Other official holidays, when government offices and post offices close but trains and buses run, the private sector often works and most shops open, are:

1 January, 20 March (Independence Day), 21 March (Youth Day), 9 April (Martyrs'

Day), 1 May, 25 July (Anniversary of the Republic), 13 August (Women's Day) and the Islamic New Year's Day.

Lost Property

There are no Lost Property offices as such, and most hotel managers let room-staff sign for and keep anything forgotten by departing guests.

(Without your own written permission room-maids and valets cannot leave work even with things you may have given them.)

Money Matters

The Tunisian dinar breaks down into millimes (thousandths) and prices are often expressed in the latter, *eg* D. 1,600 means not 1,600 dinars but one dinar 600 millimes. Coins are available in the following denominations: 1, 2, 5, 10, 20, 50 and 100 millimes, ½ and 1 dinar. There are 1, 5, 10 and 20 dinar notes in circulation.

The Tunisian authorities prohibit the import and export of their currency. They in fact fix the tourist rate weekly, and apply it nationwide: it is thus the same whether you change at the airport kiosks or hotel reception desks, certain authorised travel agencies and shops, or at banks (see **Opening Times**).

Travellers' cheques are widely negotiable. The better known credit cards are accepted in many hotels and bazaars. You should change into dinars only what you know you will need. Only 30 per cent of currency changed can be reconverted at the airport on departure – to a limit of 100 dinars, and even then only if you produce the original exchange receipts. Although many German (and some British) banks buy and sell 'smuggled' dinars at their own unarguable rates, exporting Tunisian currency is an expensive illegality.

Opening Times
During July and August most offices and banks are closed in the afternoon.
Banks Monday–Thursday 08.00–11.30hrs and 14.00–16.30hrs; Friday 08.00–11.00hrs and 13.15–15.00hrs. (From 1 July to 31 August, Monday–Friday 07.00–11.30hrs.)
Post Offices see page 120.
Shops as a guide, most shops are open 08.30–12.00hrs and 15.00–18.00hrs in winter; 08.30–12.00hrs and 16.00–19.00hrs in summer.

Personal Safety
Petty crime is plentiful, but fortunately heavy violence very rare. Hotel security is most admirable, with uniformed guards on most gates. Given the high unemployment, room-staff are usually more eager to please (by locating what you have lost) than risk their jobs by helping you lose it. But even on crowded beaches (though patrolled by mounted police in summer), unguarded towels and small possessions disappear. And you may leave your camera in an unlocked car, but the locals won't. Be wary of 'guides' offering to take

you into the medina, then demanding money to lead you out again. Women alone or in pairs are often pestered, but they are rarely harassed seriously and almost never molested (rape here carrying the death penalty). Men may be harassed by local homosexuals. Toplessness is approved in hotel grounds and tolerated on hotel beaches. Elsewhere, bikinis, briefs or low-cut blouses are not banned, but show disregard for local values.

Pharmacies
Found in all Tunisian towns and villages, the *Pharmacies* are easily recognised day and night by the Hippocratic snake in green on a large white sign. They are well stocked (and can save the cost of a doctor's visit by providing basic diagnoses, injections and changes of dressing in the backroom). Hapless travellers in isolated places often turn *in extremis* to these outposts of efficiency and sense – clean, French-speaking and with a telephone that works.
As in France, it is chemists and not gents' hairdressers that sell condoms. And though condoms are the one thing that the Tunis International Airport does not stock (because they are so cheap that departing travellers were buying up stocks), it has what every airport should have – a chemist's, or *pharmacie*.

Places of Worship
Anglican services are conducted by a resident British minister at varying times on Sundays at St George's Church

in Tunis's Place Bab Carthagène – a peaceful, sober chapel (with the tomb of the composer of 'Home Sweet Home'). Also in Sousse, Sundays at 10.00hrs at 16 Rue de Malte.

Protestant services in French are held in the Eglise réformée on the Rue Charles-de-Gaulle, Tunis, Sundays at 10.00hrs (17.00hrs Saturday – June to September).

Catholics have masses in French only: at the Jeanne d'Arc Chapel in Tunis and daily at the Cathédrale Saint-Vincent-de-Paul (08.15 and 18.30hrs, Saturday 18.00hrs and Sunday 09.00 and 11.00hrs). For times of services at French-speaking churches and chapels in other centres, ask the hotel receptionist.

Police

Policemen guard all public buildings, direct traffic, patrol streets and even (in summer) the beaches – blue-uniformed and armed, but affable and helpful.

Outside the villages and town centres, the National Guard takes over, a khaki-clad, paramilitary force responsible also for highway patrols. The effect of the latter on local road-users is such that the driver in front of you, though well within the speed limit, may stand on his brakes at the mere sight of a uniformed motor cyclist.

There are plain-clothes policemen in the tourist suqs in summer (to dampen the more tiresome salesboys' ardour) and even aboard flights by Tunis Air (an airline consequently untroubled by terrorist or hijack attempts).

Post Offices

Recognised by a yellow sign 'PTT' (the French *Poste*, *Télégraphe*, *Téléphone*), post offices open, except on public holidays, Monday to Thursday 08.00–12.00hrs and 14.00–17.00hrs hrs, Friday and Saturday 08.00–12.30hrs only (from 1 July to 31 August, Monday to Thursday 07.30–12.30hrs, with an 'emergency' service 17.00–19.00hrs – Friday and Saturday 07.30–13.30hrs).

In Tunis, the main post office on the Rue Charles-de-Gaulle is open Monday to Saturday 08.00–18.00hrs and Sunday 09.00–11.00hrs except during Ramadhan and on the three religious holidays of Mouled and the 'Ids.

Airmail cannot be relied upon for prompt delivery – certainly not as prompt as other holiday-makers just ending their stay at your hotel; if you have an urgent letter and some stamps from home, it is no bad idea to ask departing visitors to post it on their arrival home.

Public Transport

● **Air** Tunis Air operates relaxed internal services between Tunis, Monastir, Sfax, Jerba, Tozeur and Tabarka (from summer 1992). The fares are remarkably cheap but (to allow local businessmen a full day's work away) schedules tend to be late and early in the day.

● **Buses** Tunis has a good internal bus service (now complemented by a growing *métro*-tramway). Driven with exemplary patience and skill, the coaches of the (governmental) regional transport companies operate between the principal centres. Their maximum capacity is fixed in theory by law, in fact by physical possibility. The bus stations (ask for the *gare routière*) are clear and central in smaller towns; in Tunis, Sousse and Sfax they are dispersed in the general direction of their destinations.

• **Ferries** There are four to six daily ferries from Sfax to the Kerkanna Islands (1hr). From Jorf on the mainland to Ajim or Jerba every half hour during daylight (15mins).

• **Taxis** Taxis are of three kinds (or maybe four): three (passenger) seaters for the town centres and suburbs, usually Renaults or Peugeot 304s with their number on the roof; larger, rarer five-seaters, licensed for longer runs, and the 'inter-city' *louages*, usually Peugeot station-wagons. The first two types run cheaply and strictly on a meter. (The driver may need reminding to switch it on.) The rate increases by a half after 21.00hrs. In Tunis and around out-of-town hotels elsewhere they are always plentiful and empty except when you want one.

The *louages* (communal taxis) you will see waiting at their *stations* in every sizable town. You will also see them crumpled by the roadside and upside-down in ditches. They set off as soon as the authorised number of passengers has arrived to share the fixed fare ...

and the risk. Why their licences are not withdrawn for daily speeding, blind overtaking and crossing of continuous white lines is one of the mysteries of Tunisia.

The fourth putative type of taxi is what the authorities call *hippomobiles* – horse-drawn carriages, some rickety, some romantic. They ply to and from their *stations* in the main squares (save for Tunis): you decide the pace and the price.

• **Trains** Tunisia's rail services are cheap, clean, safe and comfortable, and very often punctual. First-class carriages are luxurious and even air-conditioned. The *Métro du Sahel* connects Monastir and Mahdia to the national network at Sousse. Though inland the 1,337-mile (2,151km) system

Inside Monastir's Bourguiba Mosque

was laid to cater mainly for French troops, crops and phosphates, visitors increasingly appreciate the main line between Tunis and Gabes via Hammamet, Sousse and Sfax. From Monastir and Mahdia this is joined at Sousse by the above-mentioned *Métro du Sahel*, from Nabeul via the branch line to Bir Bou Rekba (which residents of Hammamet reach by taxi).

From Tunis onward to Carthage and La Marsa runs a delightful electric railway called the Tunis, Goulette, Marsa (TGM). It is cheap and fairly frequent. From the eastern end of the Avenue Habib Bourguiba, the TGM cuts scenically across the Lake of Tunis by dyke, to stop in each of the beach suburbs. Quite apart from the sites of Carthage and Salammbo *en route*, it is the sort of train you take just for the ride.

Senior Citizens

Tunisia, in winter if not in summer, is ideal for the active elderly. Hotels offer off-season rates for long stays (and short) that compete keenly with Spain's. They also organise a less energetic programme – aerobics, bingo, cabaret and card-games – with appropriate multi-lingual patter.

European travel agencies advertise quite rightly that spending a winter here in the sun, fed and entertained in a warm hotel, is cheaper than staying at home.

Student and Youth Travel

Apart from 50 per cent off air fares for under 12s and special hotel rates for accompanied children, there are few student or youth concessions for visitors (the reductions on internal train and bus fares being reserved for students enrolled in Tunisia). Entrance is free, though, to most State museums with a student card.

Telephones

STD international code: 00, then for UK 44, for USA and Canada 1, Australia 61 and New Zealand 64. Calls from Tunisia to Europe or the States usually come through clearly. ('Automatic dialling' does not mean automatically first time; getting through by STD can be a test of patience.) Dial 17 for help from the international operator (who may for ages be otherwise engaged).

Time

Local time is Greenwich Mean Time plus one hour. Tunisia is six hours ahead of New York time.

Tipping

With labour cheap, tips are still accepted here as an incentive to better service and not, as so often in Europe, an expected payment without which there is no certainty of service at all. If service is satisfactory, 10 to 15 per cent is fairly normal for barmen and wine-waiters. Your room-maid, table-waiter and courier will be pleased with a dinar or two at the end of your stay. Two hundred millimes is good for the baggage-boy. Taxi-drivers never demand but may merit a tip.

Perhaps Tunisia's most remarkable attraction is its people: their hospitality will make any stay a memorable experience

Toilets

Impeccable, generally speaking, in tourist hotels, hotel restaurants and the international airports, and unspeakable everywhere else. If afflicted with a half-day of 'Hannibal's revenge' you should not sally forth: facilities in local cafés are guaranteed to nauseate the least squeamish, and 'comfort stops' on coach excursions are few and far between. There are no public conveniences.

All this is offset by the free access holiday-makers have to other tourist hotels. At home you might hesitate to stop at a strange hotel just for the toilet: here Europeans do so with ne'er a blush, the doorman and receptionist even showing the way.

Tourist Offices

In Tunisia:
Aïn Draham, town centre
(tel: 08 447 115)
Bizerta, 1 Rue de Constantinople
(tel: 02 432 703)
Douz, Rue Farhat Hached
(tel 05 495 341)
Gabes, Avenue Hédi Chaker
(tel: 05 270 254)
Gafsa, Place des Piscines
(tel: 06 221 664)
Hammamet, Avenue Habib
Bourguiba (tel: 02 280 423)
Houmt Souk, Rue de la
République (tel: 05 650 016/581)
Kairouan, Avenue Habib
Bourguiba (tel: 07 221 797)
Monastir, opposite Skanes
Airport (tel: 03 461 205)
Nabeul, Avenue Taïeb Mehiri
(tel: 02 286 737/800)
Nefta, Avenue Habib Bourguiba
(tel: 06 457 184)
Sfax, Place de l'Indépendance
(tel: 04 224 606)
Sousse, 1 Avenue Habib
Bourguiba (tel: 03 225 157/8)
Sousse-Nord/Port el Kantaoui

(tel: 03 231 799)
Tabarka, 32 Avenue Habib
Bourguiba (tel: 08 644 491)
Tozeur, Avenue Chabbi Abi
Elkacem (tel: 06 454 088)
Tunis, Place 7 novembre
(tel: 01 341 077)
Zarzis, Route des Hôtels
(tel: 05 680 445)
Opening times:
Monday to Thursday
08.30–17.45hrs; Friday and
Saturday 08.30–13.30hrs (July
and August 07.30–13.30hrs
and 16.00–19.00hrs); Sunday
and Public Holidays
09.00– 12.00hrs.

LANGUAGE

Common Tunisian Terms
bab door, gate
borj fort
chott salt-lake
dar house
erg sand dunes
ghorfa rock and mud
chambers
hammam Turkish bath
jami' mosque
kasba battlemented
stronghold, at highest point of
medina
marabout holy, man, who is
inhumed in a shrine also called
marabout
medersa college hostel, school
medina old town, once high-
walled, still narrow-alleyed
midha latrine/toilet of a
mosque
oued valley/river
ribat monastery-fortress
sahel coastal area
soma'a minaret of a mosque
suq market
tophet place of sacrifice

tourbet mausoleum
zawia shrine or place of prayer

Arabic phrases
Arabic is the nation's official
language. It is spoken and
written everywhere – correctly
in news broadcasts, print and
some schools, bewilderingly
elsewhere, in a babble of
unpredictable dialects that defy
grammar, syntax and often
logic, and vary from village to
village. Holiday linguists may
like to learn the few words
listed below, which will
everywhere evoke such
gratifying smiles – appreciative,
not derisory – that the effort is
worth while. If you do embark
upon anything Arabic, be
careful to falter; any show of
fluency will bring down upon
you a colloquial maelstrom,
unintelligible, embarrassing
and somewhat defeating the
object.
Far better rehearse your
French which, except for the
very young and very old in
outlying areas, everyone
understands. Or say it clearly in
English, which most hotel
employees and many
shopkeepers speak – often in
a sort of Anglo-German
esperanto.
The Arabic *kh* is the
expectoral sound that
Scotsmen end *loch* with (and
that Arabs make at their
camels). Though it may be
linguistic heresy, Arabic's
more discordant consonants,
glottal stops and the throaty
'ain and *ghain* have here been
disregarded. The heavy Arabic
h similarly requires more than a
fortnight's holiday to master.

The vowel values are given as follows: *a, e, i, o, u* as in BBC English *pat, pet, pit, poke* and *put*; *aa* as in *part*; *ai* as in *pie*; *ee* as in *pea*; *ei* as in *pay*; *ii* as in *year*; and *uu* as in *you*. Each word's stress is shown by an accent over the accentuated syllable.

Hello Ahlán, Asláama
How are you Keef el háal/Ashnooa ahwalik?
Well El hámduu liláa (Literally 'Praise be to God')
Ill, fed up, awful El hámduu liláa – Allah's omnipotence is acknowledged even when things are not good; but you may then add
No good Mish béhee
Thank you Báarak Alláahuu feek
Please Birábbee Minfadlik
I want, would like Uhíb, Habbéit
Give (me) Atée (nee)
Now/Quickly Táwa/Féessa
Today/Tomorrow Elyóm/Rúdwa
Beer/Coffee/Tea Bíira/Káhwa/Tei
Water/Milk/Bread Ma/Haléeb/Khubz
Meat/Fish/Fruit Lahm/Huut/Raláa
Butter/Sugar/Salt Zíbda/Súkar/Míleh
Hot/Warm/Cold Har/Sukhúuna/Báared
Many/Big/Small Bársha/Kebíir/Sriir
Come in/Please Tfáddal
Yes/No Naam or Aiwa/La
I/You/And Ána/Ínta/Wa
Here/There Huná/Elráadi
How much? many? Kadéish?
One/Two/Three Wáhad/Zuuz, Ithnéin/Thláatha

Four/Five/Six Árba/Khámsa/Sítta
Seven/Eight/Nine Sábaa/Thmáania/Tíssaa
Ten/Eleven/Twelve Áshra/Ihdásh/Ithnásh
Thirteen/Fourteen/Fifteen Thlaathtásh/Arbatásh/Khamstásh
Sixteen/Seventeen/Eighteen Sittásh/Sabaatásh/Thmantásh
Nineteen/Twenty Tissaatásh/Ishréen
Twenty-one/Twenty-two etc. Wáhad wa ishréen/Ithnéin wa ishréen etc.
Thirty/Forty/Fifty Thlaathéen/Arbaéen/Khamséen
Sixty/Seventy/Eighty Sittéen/Sabaéen/Thmaanéen
Ninety/Hundred/Two hundred Tissaéen/Mía/Miatéin
Three hundred/Four hundred etc. Thláatha mía/Árba mía etc.
Thousand Elf (used, too, for the dinar, *ie* '1000 millimes')
Two thousand/Three thousand etc. Elféin/Thláathat aaláaf etc.
Where is? Wein?
– **the manager** el mudíir
– **the WC** et-twalét
– **the police station** el bulées
– **the doctor** et-tabéeb
– **the chemist's** es-saidalía
– **a mechanic** garáaj
– **a telephone** teleefúun
Slow(ly) Shwei shwei
I didn't understand (you) Ma fahímt(ak)sh
If you still don't understand, just hold out for:
Left (ilal) Yesár
Right (ilal) Yeméen
(Go) Straight on (Ímshee) Tuul
Watch out! Rud báalak!
Good-bye Filamáan/Bisláama
Go away, Get lost! Ímshee, Bárra!

ACKNOWLEDGEMENTS

Acknowledgements
The Automobile Association would like to thank the following photographers and libraries for their assistance in the compilation of this book:

J ALLAN CASH PHOTO LIBRARY 103 Souvenir hunting, 105 Brass & copperware, 115 Hotel Hasdruhal.

MARY EVANS PICTURE LIBRARY 1 Fall of Carthage.

S GROSSMAN 111 Outside Mosque, 116 Camel.

INTERNATIONAL PHOTOBANK 4 Palais D'Orient, 6 Tunis, 20 Hamuda Pasha Mosque, 24 Sidi Bou Said, 63 El Jem, 72 Haumt-Souk, 76 Gabes, 81 Tozeur, 82 Nefta, 123 Shepherd.

NATURE PHOTOGRAPHERS LTD 85 Lake Ichkeul (H Miles), 87 Purple gallinule (D Hutton), 88 Swallow (K Carlson), 89 Palm dove (R Tidman), 90 Olive tree (B Burbidge), 93 Fat-tailed scorpion (S C Bisserot), 95 Blue-cheeked bee-eater (J F Reynolds).

SPECTRUM COLOUR LIBRARY Cover Hammamet, 12 Schola de Juventud, 15 Tunis Cathedral, 26/7 Souvenirs, 40/1 Camel trader, 43 Kelibia, 48 Thuburbo Maius, 49 Dougga, 66 Carpet-making, 71 Kilns, 102 Dress shop, 104 Perfume selling, 107 Hotel refreshments, 108 Entertainers, 113 Sunset, 121 Chandelier.

M TOMKINSON 16 Rue Jamaa ez-Zitouna, 29 House of the Fountain Mosaics, 30 Ghar el Melh, 33 Mosaics, 35 Hammamet beach, 37 Citrus fruit, 38 Cultural Centre, 44 El Haouaria, 46 Korbous, 53 Monastir *ribat*, 55 Sousse, 57 Monastir salt-works, 58 Martyrs' memorial, 64 Kerkenna, 74/5 Oasis, 79 Carpet weaving, 97 Fish & veg couscous, 98/9 Brik à l'oeuf, 101 *Klims*, 118 *Ojja*

ZEFA PICTURES LTD 60 Mahdia, 69 Isle of Jerba.